GERHARD WISNEW studied political science, and since 1986 has worked as an author and documentary filmmaker. The author of *One Small Step?: The Great Moon Hoax and the Race to Dominate Earth from Space*, his other bestselling books (in German) include *Das RAF-Phantom* (The RAF Phantom), *Operation 9/11*, *Mythos 9/11* and *Verschluss-Sache Terror* (The secret files of terror). The film *Das Phantom*, based on the book *Das RAF-Phantom*, was awarded the Grimme Prize in 2000.

# THE BILDERBERGERS

## PUPPET-MASTERS OF POWER?

AN INVESTIGATION INTO ALLEGATIONS OF CONSPIRACY
AT THE HEART OF POLITICS, BUSINESS AND THE MEDIA

## GERHARD WISNEWSKI

Translated by J. Collis

CLAIRVIEW

Published in Great Britain in 2014 by:
Clairview Books,
Russet, Sandy Lane,
West Hoathly,
W. Sussex RH18 5ES

E-mail: office@clairviewbooks.com

www.clairviewbooks.com

First published in 2010 under the title *Drahtzieher der Macht* by Knaur
Taschenbuch, Munich

All images are from the author's private collection or public domain, with the
exception of the following: pages 37 and 41, Ch. Kloppner and S. Mahdi and
page 48, Dorneanu

A catalogue record for this book is available from the British Library

Print book ISBN 978 1 905570 75 1
Ebook ISBN 978 1 905570 66 9

Cover by Morgan Creative featuring puppeteer image © AG Photographer and
flags image © Angelika Bentin
Typeset by DP Photosetting, Neath, West Glamorgan
Printed and bound by Gutenberg Press Ltd, Malta

'... the world is governed by very different personages from what is imagined by those who are not behind the scenes.'

*Benjamin Disraeli*
*British Prime Minister 1868 and 1874–1880*

# Contents

## Part 3

### A Global Mafia?

# Prologue

# An Encounter – Greek Style

Vouliagmeni, 17 May 2009, to the south of Athens. The sea in the bay shimmers blue, sun umbrellas on the restaurant terrace flutter lazily in the hot wind, a few teenagers splash about on the shore. A cool beer and salmon on a bed of spinach are well deserved. For days, together with a handful of journalists, I've been chasing after participants at the Bilderberg Conference and letting myself in for a sometimes more, sometimes less amusing game of hide-and-seek with security personnel and police. I'm about to order another beer when my mobile rings. A colleague is telling me that he and the other journalists have just been released from police custody after hours of interrogation. He's in our hotel lobby and I'd better come over straight away.

No more relaxing, then. I pay and leave the terrace via the exit to the street. Just as I'm about to set off for the crossing in the direction of the hotel, I notice two policemen standing there, pointing towards me. As inconspicuously as possible I return to the terrace by the next entrance, switch off my mobile and lock myself in the toilet for half an hour. When nothing happens I leave the restaurant again, this time by the main entrance. On the opposite side of the street a steep stone stairway leads up and over towards the hotel. Surely I can get to it without having to pass the police presence at the crossing, I think. Ten seconds later I'm panting my way up the exceedingly steep stairs. I'm nearly at the top and watching my step when I suddenly glimpse two female feet dangling idly from the parapet. Somehow they remind me of Kaa the snake in the *Jungle Book* lying in wait for Mowgli. I've scarcely reached her when she says 'Hello' in English as I pause for breath: 'Where are you from?' Germany, I say. 'Oh, yes? Germany!' Quite by chance her father lives there, or her brother or a nephew.

A Greek woman all alone accosting strange men at the top of a steep flight of steps? Hang on, I think. She is, moreover, nothing like other charming young Greek women tripping around here in their high heels. She's a rather more austere, sporty type — not unattractive, no, but austere, without make-up and with short hair, obviously dyed blonde.

I ask if she happens to know Litous Street, which is where my hotel is. Oh! Litous Street, sure, she replies eagerly. I'd have to go back down the steps and turn right. She'll come with me and show me the way! Just a minute — so she wants to escort me directly to her colleagues. Well, no, I declare jokingly, sounding like a harmless tourist, I haven't struggled all the way up these stairs only to turn round and go down again. I'll carry on over this hill to my hotel. She rather sees the point, but just then a sporty young man appears from nowhere and settles down, smiling, beside her on the low wall. Our little chat now develops into an interrogation: What am I doing here? What's my 'job'? She comes to the point immediately. 'Are you a journalist?'

A journalist? Me? 'No', I reply. 'No?' she repeats. 'No!' I also repeat. Had I heard about the conference, she persists. 'What conference?' I ask, sounding decidedly nonchalant. Well, the Bilderberg Conference of course, she says. Bilderberg? 'Never heard of it', I counter. 'What kind of a conference is it, then?' I want to know, but she doesn't want to tell me. Well, the one in the Nafsika Astir Palace. That's the conference hotel, is it, I conjecture vaguely. 'Yes', she confirms. But what's my job, she insists. 'Political scientist', I say. Ah! *Political science* and Bilderberg; this combination is a wake-up call to her police-woman's brain. What do you do, then, in *political science*? 'I write', I reply. Wrong again. The effect is like dangling a mouse in front of a cat. *Political science* and *writing* — this appears to be the greatest crime one can commit in the vicinity of the Bilderbergers. The street might as well be full of signs saying 'Writing forbidden!' And of course 'Thinking forbidden!' and 'No questions!' So what did I write about, then? 'Marxism', I say, choosing the most uninteresting answer possible as I turn to leave. I block off further questions with a 'Nice to have met you'. Such a pleasant little chat by the wayside.

# Introduction

Many things can be found on the internet. For example that there's a power group which meets once a year known as the 'Bilderbergers'. This club is supposed to be much mightier than any government or even the G8 Summit, that annual meeting of eight global giants. If the latter amounts to a circle of elephants, then the Bilderbergers must be a whole herd, 100 to 150 personages: former and future US Presidents, former and current NATO General Secretaries, former and current CEOs, current, and above all future, German Chancellors! From Germany, for example, Josef Ackermann, Joschka Fischer, Guido Westerwelle, Wolfgang Schäuble and Otto Schily. But also Kurt Georg Kiesinger, Willy Brandt, Helmut Schmidt, Helmut Kohl and Angela Merkel!

Any number of heavyweights, then. And, if one believes the internet, these heavyweights are supposed to belong to a kind of world government. According to some, indeed, to 'the' world government. Whatever the case may be, it is interesting to note that while the G8 circle of elephants gallops loudly across the media landscape once a year, the shadows of the Bilderberg pachyderms tiptoe around in silence. Not a word is breathed by the media about them, or if they do come up once in a while, then only as an aside.

So our first reaction has to be one of suspicion: Does this summit really exist? And if so, does it actually have anything important to say?

One hears that this 'secret world government' meets annually at different locations around the world in order to discuss, behind closed doors, questions that involve all of us. And because it is indeed significant for all of us when industry bosses meet behind closed doors with ministers, with the military, with monarchs and with international puppet-masters, I decide to get to the bottom of this matter. I will ferret out this secretive annual 'Bilderberg' Conference which is said to be much older than the G8 Summit and indeed even the European Union. I shall take up the trail at the Bilderbergers' first conference hotel where this secret group is said to have been founded over half a century ago, in 1954. Then I shall visit one of the more recent conference hotels, where the Bilderbergers met in Germany in 2005, and endeavour to elicit some information from the hotel's director. And finally I'll make my way to a current Bilderberg Conference in Athens in order to find out how secretive these conferences really still are and how difficult it is to contact any of the participants.

On my return I shall continue to follow the trail in the relevant literature and look into the origins and background of the Bilderbergers. In doing this I'll discover that they were founded in 1954 but also that in reality they are merely a subsection of a much more ancient world power. And finally I will myself approach at least the German participants in the Conferences and circulate a short questionnaire among the select band of almost fifty German Bilderbergers. I want to know the purpose of this whole affair, what is discussed during those conferences, and what those questioned consider to be the purpose of it all.

Depending on their answers or non-answers, I shall then look more closely at a number of the Bilderbergers and endeavour to size them up on the basis of what they have done during their membership: What projects or initiatives did they set in train during that period? Did they perhaps found a new large company? Or start a war? In the end I will succeed in gaining some insight into one of the conferences. By examining the lectures given we shall discover the true plans of the Bilderbergers and realize that these plans conform exactly with our prior investigations of individual participants. This will complete our picture of the group and we shall then be able to identify the threat posed by this secret conference.

# Part 1

# TRACKING DOWN THE BILDERBERGERS

# The Dorint Sofitel beside Lake Tegernsee

Tegernsee, 6 May 2005. The medics are at it again! As reported by a daily newspaper, a medical congress is taking place at the luxury Dorint hotel at Rottach-Egern. But you'll search in vain for a stethoscope or a medical bag among the participants. In fact it's not a question of medics at all. That's a disguise. The supposed medical congress is actually a meeting of the world government. Or at least so the fault-finders say, the critics of the 'Bilderberg' group which actually derives its name from its very first venue.

At the end of April 2005 the staff at this exclusive hotel experienced an encounter of the third kind. Quite some time previously an international company had booked the entire establishment for a three-day period. And now that company came clean to the management regarding the actual participants: the Bilderbergers.

26 November 2006. Bright sunshine, an unusually warm autumn day. The cars are grinding to a halt in the narrow Tegernsee valley which is surrounded by mountains and might be compared to a funnel – or a natural fort. From above, arriving from Munich, you drive downwards until the mountains close in around you. And at the bottom, to the south, there is only one narrow exit, in the direction of Austria. Rottach-Egern is situated beside this exit. This is the location of one of Germany's most expensive hotels, formerly the Dorint Sofitel, Seehotel Überfahrt Tegernsee.

'The whole valley was full of police', the hotel's General Director B. remembers. And there were all kinds of security measures within the hotel itself; but B. doesn't want to be any more specific than that.

I meet him in the lobby bar. Hushed music and hushed conversations accompanied by the gentle splash of a large fountain beneath a sign displaying the name of the hotel. I've come because I want to know whether the Bilderbergers actually exist at all – or whether they are nothing more than a phantom spooking about in the internet, consisting of a few rumours, forum entries and out-of-focus photos. I've come because some of those unclear pictures were taken here in front of the hotel's main entrance: They show the then president of the World Bank, James D. Wolfensohn, the American milliardaire[*] David Rockefeller, and Jaap de Hoop Scheffer, General Secretary of NATO. I want to know whether the most powerful people on earth really do gather in private once a year in order to take charge of the world's fate. 'Yes, those pictures were taken here', says General Director B., a tall, handsome man in his mid-forties, with greying hair. His expression is frank, somewhat boyish even, if not mischievous. The reason why so few photos of the grandees of world politics were taken at this spot is that there is a large, secluded park at the back of the hotel where most of the Bilderbergers strolled when they wanted to stretch their legs.

The Bilderberg club has been touring the world for 60 years. It appears out of thin air, takes over an entire luxury hotel and then disappears again without trace. Not a word escapes from its meetings apart from a condescending press release after a day or two, giving the names of the participants and some vaguely formulated discussion topics. That's it. The Bilderbergers will never return: 'The Bilderbergers', says General Director B., 'are a once in a lifetime experience.' Between 5 and 8 May 2005, while they were conferring in his hotel, even he and his staff were locked out of the meeting rooms.

B. is above such things; he knows his limits. He doesn't allow journalists to make him nervous, but he prevents them from becoming too inquisitive by giving a hint here and there. He does not refuse point blank to answer any questions at all but he won't be pushed beyond a certain point, one which he determines himself. He can chat about the Bilderbergers for three quarters of an hour

---

[*] Milliard = billion, or one thousand million.

without giving away any great secrets. But trifling ones, yes. Sure, once in a while forgotten conference papers had been left lying around – but not a word about their content passes his lips. By comparison with other conferences, I ask him, are the topics discussed by the Bilderbergers merely a lot of hot air, or are they purposeful? 'Purposeful', he replies curtly. So it's not a matter of a nice party of the elite exchanging first names and business cards. It's a matter of taking decisions. 'These people are impatient', B. discloses. Impatient? 'I can give you a tip: Keep an eye on the media over the first four to six weeks after a Bilderberg Conference, and watch what happens.' Any details? No, no. Just see generally who loses his job and who gets taken on, which companies are bought and which are sold, who gets elected and who loses out.

Letting my thoughts wander for a moment, I think back to May 2005. The Bilderberg Conference beside Lake Tegernsee took place from 5 to 8 May. But what else happened? Was there anything else? Suddenly I remember: On 22 May, entirely out of keeping with his intentions thus far, German Federal Chancellor Gerhard Schröder surprisingly announced new elections, which it was only possible to set in train so quickly by applying dodgy constitutional stratagems. Six months later Angela Merkel became Chancellor. So what? Was Schröder a guest at the Bilderberg Conference? Reports say yes – but only for a few minutes. According to rumours: in order to collect the papers. I shall return to this later. And what else? Was Angela Merkel a guest at the conference? Oh, yes – and for rather longer than five minutes. And four months after that she was elected Federal Chancellor. I am beginning to believe that B. is right. I shall scrutinize the weeks following Bilderberg meetings more closely.

We now come to another topic. If we compare these meetings with those of the G8 Summit, do we perhaps gain the impression that the latter are nothing more than distractions while the serious stuff is played out at the meetings of the Bilderbergers? B. squirms a bit, but says nothing, though at least he doesn't contradict me. I suddenly realize: The G8 Summits and other public events are nothing other than brightly-lit circus arenas in which bridled political performers show off their tricks. Presidents, Federal Chancellors, Prime Ministers are nothing more than circus horses. The ringmasters are elsewhere. They are the Bilderbergers or, more exactly, their hard core.

B. says nothing, but he sees that I have understood. Bright lights shine and cameras click where the circus horses prance. But it's pitch dark where the ringmasters meet: no camera teams, no press conferences, no interviews. Nothing. Or have you ever seen a meeting of ringmasters taking place in a circus arena? Of course not. The Bilderbergers hold their meetings as though in the backroom of our media society. And things become critical when the circus horses suddenly want to play at being ringmasters: 'In view of certain scandalous cases, an independent observer might well reach the conclusion that the victim in question was obliged to lose his life for the very reason that, although he was a member of the elite circle, as time went on he chose either consciously or unconsciously to oppose its aims', speculates author and Bilderberg observer Andreas von Rétyi. 'Murders of this kind have also befallen Bilderbergers, murders that have never been solved nor the perpetrators found.'

There have indeed been several mysterious deaths among the Bilderbergers. Think of people like Alfred Herrhausen. The Director of Deutsche Bank was personally invited to Bilderberg meetings. 'Herrhausen had presented the Bilderberg Conference, an influential and elite circle of politicians and industry leaders from all over the world, with some truly heretical suggestions,' wrote *Der Spiegel* on 3 October 1988 in one of those quite casual mentions of the conference: 'The banker recommended that participants should consider the matter of a debt reduction for the third world.' As time went on the conflict about the debt reduction became increasingly bitter, especially between Deutsche Bank and some American finance institutions. About a year after the report in *Der Spiegel*, the banker was dead. He was suddenly murdered by 'terrorists' on 30

November 1989. The perpetrators have never been caught. Can there be any connection? Other Bilderbergers have also been killed, for example the boss of Dresdner Bank, Jürgen Ponto, murdered by 'terrorists' on 30 July 1977. Or Swedish Prime Minister Olof Palme, shot by an unknown killer on 28 February 1986. That culprit has also never been caught.

The air at the Dorint Sofitel suddenly feels bitterly cold; I order a coffee. 'Mmm, the air up there is thin,' says B., seemingly guessing my thoughts. 'Even I feel it to some extent as the director of this hotel.' Business cards go out of date quickly – his says 'Deputy Director'. Yet he's already the General Director.

You feel the power these people have, says General Director B. And however unclear this whole thing is, the manager of this hotel, who moves among alpha men on a daily basis, is in no doubt at all as to the identity of the leader of the pack: 'Kissinger'. Even though he's so small – uncannily small. Yes, I say, like Napoleon. B. laughs. I want to know more about Kissinger's influence. B. blocks. We're back at his professional limit: no details. Despite this I note: Kissinger is the boss, the others are more likely to take orders. Apart from certain exceptions, such as David Rockefeller, who has been Kissinger's friend and mentor for decades.

I take my leave of Director B. and of the Dorint; in 2007 B. was made Director of the Dorint in the Baltic resort of Wustrow. A final look at the hall and the splashing, halogen-illuminated fountain. I'm still in the early days of my investigations, but I already know that the Bilderbergers really do exist. And I have breathed the same air – air that feels somewhat chilly.

# Hotel De Bilderberg

Bilderberg: what an odd name. Initially I couldn't imagine what it meant. Until I discovered that it was the name of the hotel at which this global elite had held its first ever conference: the Hotel De Bilderberg at Oosterbeek in Holland. So off I went to Oosterbeek. Not because I expected to find any great secrets still lurking there, but because I was a victim of that sense of unreality engendered by the total lack of any kind of reporting. The Bilderbergers felt like something virtual, almost resembling an organization in a novel, and I wanted to rid myself of this feeling. So one fine summer's day I extended a business trip to Düsseldorf northwards to Arnhem in Holland, of which Oosterbeek is a suburb. You drive northwards along the A57 towards Duisburg, Goch and Cleves where the landscape becomes ever flatter, flat as a pancake, interrupted only by geometrically laid out poplar groves. After passing the Hanseatic city of Nijmegen you carry on towards Arnhem, site of one of the last Allied defeats in World War II. The Rhine crossing was fought over bitterly here. In September 1944 the Allied military operation Market Garden failed in the face of fierce German opposition.

Today Arnhem bears little resemblance to the pretty post-card scenes found on Google Images. Combined with Nijmegen it's more of a great conurbation with 700,000 inhabitants, an uncouth urban landscape with concrete viaducts and bizarre multi-coloured high-rises. Two pale blue to pale green tower-blocks stand out; like New York's twin towers, they also house a World Trade Centre. I wind my way to Oosterbeek through the city chaos. Whether intention-ally or not, the choice of a suburb of Arnhem for the location of the first Bilderberg Conference feels significant. In World War II the Allies had important headquarters here in their battle against Ger-many and for the globalized world which emerged from that war.

The British general Robert 'Roy' Urquhart, for example, who commanded the British First Airborne Division during the battle for the Rhine bridges, lodged at the Hartenstein Hotel, an old villa at Utrechtsweg 232 which is now an aviation museum. Another high-class villa on Utrechtsweg (no. 261 today) was the generously proportioned De Bilderberg country house. Built in 1918 in the midst of a beautifully wooded area, the property changed hands several times before being purchased by the hotel company De Tafelberg in 1925. Baths were installed in the bedrooms, and in the spring of 1926 the De Bilderberg Hotel opened for guests. Its capacity was doubled in 1933. During the battle for Arnhem and its bridges in September 1944 the De Bilderberg found itself between two fronts. Occupied by the Germans on 5 September, it was con-siderably damaged during the ensuing battles. Nevertheless, as it was still the largest building in the area it was from there that the post-war reconstruction measures were organized. In 1946 half the building reopened as a hotel with makeshift furnishings.

When I arrived at the Utrechtsweg in 2008 my impression was

*The hotel's sign at the roadside*

*Carpark for guests*

that the De Bilderberg still values its seclusion. I drove along the street from Oosterbeek towards Doorwerth and back several times without finding any trace of it. I was about to give up when I noticed its 'camouflaged' signboard amongst the trees. A brown notice among brown tree trunks. You could hardly do a better job of hiding it, I thought. But is camouflage really the deeper purpose of a lodging such as this? Not really. So as I drove slowly up the narrow lane to the hotel complex I decided I'd have to give the management a hint about matters of marketing.

But that was a plan I immediately abandoned when I saw the hotel's carpark: row upon row of Dutch cars with bike racks on the back. Today, Hotel De Bilderberg is a favourite destination for cyclists looking for relaxation on their two-wheeled steeds. The hotel itself is an extended two-story complex with characteristic front-facing gables.

With its glass annexes and old winter-garden it has a whiff of the 'magic mountain'. And in the interior, history and tradition are much in evidence. In part the furnishings might still belong to the

*A Chess game of the old world-order: The Hotel De Bilderberg – starting point of the Bilderberg conspiracy*

1950s when David Rockefeller and Prince Bernhard of the Netherlands shook hands here in their bid to transform the military commander's hill on Utrechtsweg into a civilian one. You can picture the industrial directors of the economic miracle seated at the long conference table of burnished wood while animated ladies chat in the brightly-lit winter-garden with its impressive bar rather reminiscent of Stanley Kubrick's *The Shining*.

Since the De Bilderberg is now a family hotel for (rather wealthy) day-trippers, the conference table looks positively antediluvian. Hardly anyone in today's hotel trade is interested in the establishment's history. But for the few who are inquisitive enough to ask, the reception desk does hand out an A4 page of information which even has a paragraph about the Bilderberg Conference:

> The first Bilderberg Conference was held at the De Bilderberg Hotel in 1954. About one hundred influential heads of state, heads of government and industrialists were present. The aim of the Bilderberg Conference was to improve the strained

*The old conference table at Hotel De Bilderberg*

*The winter-garden at Hotel De Bilderberg*

relationship between Europe and America. The meeting was not public. . . . The initiator of the conference was Dr. Joseph H. Retinger from Poland who travelled a great deal in Europe and was acquainted with every important individual in Western Europe. Among others, he initiated collaboration with Prince Bernhard, who participated in the first conference and subsequently became the permanent chairman, a position he held until 1976. The success of the first Bilderberg Conference was such that the organizers decided to continue the conferences.

Even in those days, over half a century ago, the place was 'surrounded by guards, so that no journalist could approach within a kilometre of the hotel', the information sheet declares.

Unbelievable! And what of nowadays?

# All's quiet at the Bilderberg summit

Summer 2007: Everyone is talking about the G8 Summit at Heiligendamm in Germany. While the location is surrounded for the
duration of the meeting, from 6 to 8 June, by 16,000 police, 2,000
journalists and tens of thousands of anti-globalization protesters,
the really important summit remains in the dark. Whereas at
Heiligendamm cudgels twitch, water-cannon spurt and the whole
nation is hypnotized via the TV by the battles raging around the G8
Summit, not a single critic of globalization, not a single demon-
strator and not a single journalist shows any interest in another
summit of a very specific kind taking place quite nearby in time,
although far away geographically: the Bilderberg summit in Istanbul, from 31 May to 3 June. That's strange, since not merely eight,
but over seventy heavyweights of world politics are attending the
meeting at the Ritz Carlton Hotel there. A few days later, at Heiligendamm, it's mainly figureheads like George W. Bush and Angela
Merkel who meet, whereas in Istanbul it's the globalizers themselves who are involved. And yet: no-one at all pays any attention to
it. The Bilderberg summit remains unmentioned in editors' travel
plans and ducks beneath the radar of any public awareness. The
international media have used up their travel budgets and allocated
their personnel ready for the G8 Summit from 6 to 8 June and can't
possibly trek to a summit elsewhere which no-one knows about, of
which no-one has ever heard and where they would anyway not be
welcome. While the G8 circus opens its doors at Heiligendamm, its
ringmasters, protected by the media racket, meet elsewhere. TV
viewers are left empty-handed as they gape at the wrong summit,
which they regard as democratic openness: all those supposed
debates among the participants, the discussion and passing of all
kinds of papers, and above all the struggling and wrestling and

struggling again. He who 'struggles' and fights is the one who identifies with the problems. That's what the electors are supposed to believe. Unlike the G8 Summit, where the organizers hold the public in thrall with whole bundles of excitement, from climate catastrophes to aid for Africa, not a word escapes from the Bilderberg cogitations apart from the brief accounts already mentioned. And even these rarely receive a mention in the media. All's quiet at the Bilderberg summit.

## A non-contact office at Leiden

How can it be that you have never heard anything about the Bilderbergers? Well, it's because the Bilderbergers don't want you to hear about them. Whereas by now every local bakery has its own internet page, you'll search in vain for a Bilderberg website.[*] Unlike the G8 Summit, which marches through the global media village with much beating of drums months before the date of a meeting, the Bilderberg summit has no website, no e-mail address, in fact not even a postal address. Only a post-office box with the number 3017 at Leiden in Holland; and also a telephone and fax number. But this doesn't enable you to make contact, for it's a non-contact office. Or rather, it's a lock. An air-lock. A lock is a connecting passage which joins two incompatible spaces. Surely you've heard of air-locks in high-security bio-research laboratories where you can only open one door after the previous one has been closed? This is the type of quarantine that surrounds the Bilderbergers. The air they breathe is cold and thin – unbelievably thin and probably not appropriate for ordinary mortals. And the air-lock which ensures that Bilderbergers and the media do not breathe even a cubic centimetre of the same air is that office at Leiden whence a woman named Maja B. passes,

---

[*] This was the case in 2010, when the German edition of this book was first published. There is now a modest official website at www.bilderbergmeetings.org

or rather does not pass, information to the public. At an exactly specified moment she hands out two things from the Bilderberg world: the usual notice to the media and the list of participants. Both serve one purpose above all: to ensure that at least formally a Bilderberg Conference cannot be described as a 'secret event'. None of the media will put out reports since the Bilderbergers will ensure by other means that this won't happen. As we know, what doesn't appear on TV doesn't exist, while what does appear does exist: Saddam Hussein's weapons of mass destruction, Osama bin Laden, climate catastrophe and more. I flicker and therefore I am. Again I'm assailed by that sense of unreality. That discrete Bilderberg woman with the charm of a robot sends out nothing, of course. The air-lock is a one-way street. Participation? Interviews? Of course not.

### A book never published

The mass media are not alone in revealing nothing. Projected books about the Bilderbergers, too, crash at the last moment, even when they are already listed in booksellers' catalogues. You can examine an index-corpse of this kind on amazon.com. In 2002 the prize-winning American author and journalist Renata Adler wanted to publish a book about the 'Private Capacity' of the Bilderbergers. According to the catalogue, it was to be 'the first serious investigation of the ultra-clandestine Bilderberg Conferences and their role in the modern world'.[1] 'This book deals for the first time with the true story of the organization, its participants and their activities ... It explains how the Bilderbergers themselves have changed and in what way they may have changed the world.' This was still there for all to read on amazon.com in 2007.[*] And how very much one would have liked to read that book! But it was not to be. The book couldn't

---

[*] At time of publication (September 2014), the title and blurb can be viewed on www.amazon.co.uk under the ISBN 9781891620904.

be ordered, yet today it still lurks in the internet. The English Wikipedia entry for Renata Adler has: '*In Private Capacity: The History of the Bilderberg Conference*. 320 pages, Time Warner Paperbacks (5 Sep 2002). ISBN 0-316-85545-6.'

A Bilderberg book never published: In Private Capacity *by Renata Adler*

So what happened next? In answer to a query from Andreas Bummel, an author with the Internet News Service Telepolis, the director of communications at Public Affairs, a branch of Perseus Books, replied: 'In a conversation with our publisher I was told that on the basis of an agreement between the author Renata Adler and the publisher, Public Affairs, it was decided to refrain from pub- lishing *In Private Capacity*.' (Telepolis, 13.8.2003)

How strange! But the reason given for this waiver is even stran- ger: 'Although author and publisher agreed that the subject of the suggested book was fascinating, both parties were also of the opinion that devoting a whole book to it would probably not be necessary. In the publishing business it often turns out that what looks like a great idea for a book can be better dealt with in a shorter form, for example a magazine article'. (Ibid.)

A book about a club of over one hundred top globalists which has been meeting for half a century is 'not necessary'? Andreas Bummel agrees that this explanation 'is unfortunately not very convincing'. In fact it is plausible at most for non-experts, which makes it even more mysterious. In reality a publishing company will consider a book well in advance of any contractual agreement, and certainly before the work is included in any catalogue. If this were not the case, catalogues would be full of book projects about which publishers have subsequently changed their minds. In reality the procedure in this case amounts to a curious one-off instance reeking suspiciously of slamming on the brakes.

Some books about the Bilderbergers have meanwhile been written, but not by insiders. It is unlikely that the authors were in a position of being able to enter the Bilderberg world through the airlock. Perhaps some scrap or other, or the odd quotation, has managed to escape through that sterile passage. Bilderberg pachyderms such as Henry Kissinger do on occasion scatter a few such crumbs, but it is difficult for Bilderberg astrologers to glean sufficient nourishment from them.

Renata Adler has an honorary doctorate from Georgetown University (the oldest Jesuit university in the US, see later) and thus has been honoured by the establishment. She had other ideas. It was stated in the book's presentation that leading Bilderbergers had passed the club's archive to her. It had been her intention to describe the organization with the help of that archive. Undoubtedly a good catch for a journalist – rather too good, perhaps.

### The conspiracy of silence

Did I say earlier that the media were not welcomed by the Bilderbergers? Actually that's not quite true. In fact they are extremely welcome – but only some of them. And then only if they say absolutely nothing at all. For example the founder and president of Perseus Books, the publisher involved with Renata Adler's book, Frank H. Pearl. According to Telepolis he was a participant at the Bilderberg Conferences during the very years before and during which Adler's book was to have been published, in 2001 and 2002. (Telepolis, ibid.) To think ill of this doesn't make you a cynic.

Yet Frank H. Pearl is only a small fish. You'd be surprised to discover who else takes part in those conferences: namely the very media moguls to whom you entrust your soul on a daily basis. The saying 'Lord, into thine hands do I commend my spirit' ought long since to have been recast to say: 'Lord Springer, or Lord Döpfner, into your hands do I commend my spirit.' Although the founder of the Axel Springer publishing company has been dead for some years, the Springer Conglomerate (*Bild, Die Welt, Hörzu, Hamburger Abendblatt, AutoBild* etc.) has, of course, long since been run by others, such as the said Mr Döpfner. And he, for example, was a guest at the Bilderberg Conference in 2005 and 2006. Now, wouldn't an insider-report about the Bilderberg Conference be sensational for the millions who read *Bild, Die Welt* and all those other papers! However, Mr. Döpfner never did deliver that insider report. Instead – or rather therefore – in 2007 he was awarded a prize, namely the Leo-Baeck-Medal, 'named after the liberal German rabbi Leo Baeck' (Wikipedia). The same prize was also awarded to 'Bilderbergers' James D. Wolfensohn, Otto Schily and Joschka Fischer.

The Springer conglomerate is a strategic media company, one of the huge emotional and informational catapults of the world which for some time now has been increasing in size in order to bombard ever larger areas of the globe with its opinions. For it is opinions, above all the correct opinions, which are so immeasurably valuable. So Springer has been expanding its umbrella of influence across the world, beginning with France, Spain and Switzerland, via Poland, Hungary and the Czech Republic right over to Russia and China. The journal *AutoBild* alone is sold in thirty countries, thus reaching, according to an announcement to the press by the Axel Springer AG on 12 April 2007, a readership of forty million. There are also numerous offshoots of the *Bild* newspaper,* spreading the same bad

---

* *Bild Zeitung* (or, literally, 'picture newspaper') is a populist 'tabloid' German daily.

taste wherever they appear, for example in Poland. In the run-up to the European football championship game between Germany and Poland in 2008, the Polish 'Bild' with its glossy title *Fakt* depicted the Polish national trainer as a knight in full armour raising his sword to execute the German footballer Michael Ballack. At the same time, on the other bank of the river Oder, the German *Bild* newspaper expressed its anger about the report – without mentioning that *Fakt* is also a Springer product (see shortnews.de, 6.6.2008). According to the Axel Springer Publishing Company's website (7.4.2009), its extensive media portfolio includes, in addition to the *Bild* and *Die Welt* group, more than 170 newspapers and journals, over 60 online offerings, and collaboration with TV and radio broadcasters in 35 countries. This shows the extent of the power packaged in just one Bilderberg figure. Yet these 170 rags will have little to report about the Bilderberg Conferences.

Another frequent guest of the Bilderbergers is the powerful publisher Hubert Burda who brings out opinion-forming papers such as *Focus*, which is a kind of *Der Spiegel* for the poor, and also *Die Bunte, Neue Woche, Super Illu* and *Playboy*. As is the case with Springer, Burda also decides, through his papers *TV Spielfilm, TV Today, TV Schlau, TV Spielfilm XXL*, what millions are to watch on television. The Burda publishing company brings out about 260 titles in 27 countries. These, too, are not likely to write much about the Bilderbergers.

*Die Zeit*, the German *Bild* newspaper for intellectuals, is also firmly anchored among the Bilderbergers, namely through its publisher Josef Joffe, its former publisher Theo Sommer and its temporary chief editor Matthias Nass. The latter appears to feel especially comfortable among the Bilderbergers, having visited them up to eleven times. Joffe has been taking part in forming German opinion for decades; before he joined *Die Zeit* he was foreign policy boss at *Süddeutsche Zeitung*.

The fact is that the presence of the media among the Bilderbergers generates less, not more, information for the public. Present among the participants at the 2007 Conference in Istanbul were leading representatives of the following media or media conglomerates:

| | |
|---|---|
| *Le Figaro* | France |
| Hubert Burda Media Holdings | Belgium |
| Grupo PRISA media group | Spain |
| *The Wall Street Journal* | USA |
| The Washington Post Company | USA |
| *Die Zeit* | Germany |
| *The Times* | Great Britain |
| Yeni Safak | Turkey |
| | |
| Indigo Books & Music Inc. | Canada |
| *Politiken* | Denmark |
| *International Herald Tribune* | USA |
| *The Financial Times* | Great Britain |
| *The Economist* | Great Britain |

Who would have thought it! Representatives of the same media that spew forth more than enough on the G8 Summit! Yet they publish scarcely a word about the Bilderberg Conference they have themselves attended. This is a fact. At the 1991 Bilderberg Conference in Baden-Baden, Rockefeller is said to have explicitly thanked the media for their silence: 'We are grateful to *The Washington Post, The New York Times, Time* magazine and other great publications whose directors have attended our meetings and respected their promises of discretion for almost forty years.' This is how Rockefeller is quoted in almost every source about the Bilderbergers: 'It would have been impossible for us to develop our plan for the world if we had been subject to the bright lights of publicity during those years. But, the world is now much more sophisticated and prepared to march towards a world government. The supranational sovereignty of an intellectual elite and world bankers is surely preferable to the national auto-determination practiced in past centuries.' However:

this is not confirmed, notes author Will Banyan in his essay *The Proud Internationalist*,[2] which deals in detail with the origin of the quote. I, too, have a feeling that it is rather too heavy-handed. But on the other hand, Rockefeller is actually quite capable of forthright comment, as we shall see at the end of this book.

## A top-level clique

What is true is that every year the American milliardaire David Rockefeller brings together about one hundred of his closest friends, cronies and business associates for a meeting with global enablers who then get going politically. David Rockefeller is the pike in the fish-pond of the American *imperium* and one of the leading figures on the planet – patriarch of leading worldwide dynasties, (former) finance tycoon, global statesman, friend of the secret service and head of the Rockefeller empire (to which Standard Oil, Chase Manhattan Bank and others used to belong). We are familiar with most of his buddies from the headlines, and they used to be found or still are found at the Bilderberg meetings: Henry A. Kissinger (former US Secretary of State and presidential adviser), James D. Wolfensohn (ex-World Bank President), Henry R. Kravis (Private Equity Investor), Paul Volcker (ex-Chase Manhattan, ex-Federal Reserve President), Gianni Agnelli (former Managing Director of Fiat), Nelson Mandela, Kofi Annan (ex-UN General Secretary), Colin Powell (ex-US Chief of Staff and ex-Secretary of State), Zbigniew Brzezinski (former security adviser and geostrategist), Henry Ford II (industry tycoon), Richard Helms and Allen Dulles (ex-CIA chiefs), John F. Kennedy, Jimmy Carter (former US Presidents), and so on. We lack both time and space for an exhaustive chronicle of the Rockefeller universe as a whole.

The list of participants at the 2007 Bilderberg Conference includes:

Henry A. Kissinger (see above)

Richard Perle, ultra-rightwing presidential adviser

Richard N. Haass, Chairman of the omnipotent Council on Foreign Relations (CFR; USA)

Timothy F. Geithner, former president of US Central Bank Federal Reserve, now US Finance Minister under Barack Obama

Robert B. Zoellick, President of the World Bank

Jean-Claude Trichet, boss of the European Central Bank

Jaap de Hoop Scheffer, NATO General Secretary

Peter D. Sutherland, Chairman of Goldman Sachs

Vernon E. Jordan, Senior Managing Director, Lazard Frères

James D. Wolfensohn, ex-World Bank President

... among others.

G8 stars such as Angela Merkel, or before her Gerhard Schröder, are no more than foot soldiers in the circle of these world leaders. While they delude us into crediting them with leadership, the real music is actually being performed elsewhere.

## Aristocracy and financial aristocracy

Any more questions? Of course. Namely: Why is there so much talk about 'aristocracy and financial aristocracy' in connection with the Bilderbergers? It's obvious: In addition to finance, industry, energy, the military, politics, governments and media among the Bilderbergers, it would be wrong to ignore a further group, namely the aristocracy and also royalty. Bankers such as Rockefeller and Rothschild have always supplied rulers with the stuff of power, namely money. And those who imagine that monarchies have lost their worldly power find themselves mistaken in the context of the Bilderbergers, where the royals exercise their might entirely unofficially. One of the Bilderberg co-founders was, for example, Prince

Bernhard of the Netherlands, father of Queen Beatrix who herself also became a permanent Bilderberg participant. Further royal guests are Prince Philippe of Belgium, and Prince Philip, Duke of Edinburgh, consort of Queen Elizabeth II of England, Australia, New Zealand and several other Commonwealth countries. Well, royalty, whether of Spain or England, has always played the leading role in colonization, and this is no different nowadays, only now we call it globalization. The colony is now not an individual country but the world as a whole. Thus Sofia, Queen of Spain, also frequently joins Beatrix, Queen of the Netherlands, at Bilderberg meetings. According to a report in *The Guardian* of 28 April 1986, Prince Charles was seen at the Bilderberg Conference in Scotland. After all, members of royal houses are not only among the wealthiest individuals on the planet but also often leading figures in industry and commerce, for example in the case of the appropriately titled Royal Dutch Shell.

## Globalization = Colonization

Colonization has always been accompanied and promoted by standardization. The abolition of borders and the standardization of laws and currencies make it easier to influence and exploit colonies. Projects such as the European Union, concocted by none other than the Bilderbergers, should also be viewed in this light. 'I believe it can be said that the Treaties of Rome, which initiated the Common Market, were born during those meetings', Bilderberger George McGhee is said to have admitted. The United States of course also came into existence on the basis of British colonies. And after World War II, the USA and Great Britain formed a new *de facto* Anglo-American world empire. And since 11 September 2001 they have been inaugurating a new colonization, pardon: a new globalization project under the guise of the 'war on terror' and the 'clash of civilizations'. As we can all see, the United Kingdom and the

'United Colonies' of America are world leaders in matters of 'globalization'. And the only reasons for the United Kingdom not being a full member of the European Union are: firstly it does not want to become attached to a potential colony, and secondly because it is opposed to the break-up now threatening the other member states of the EU.

# 'Look out for three sozzled Americans!' —
# In the hornets' nest of the Bilderbergers

As I wanted to know what happens nowadays during a Bilderberg summit I sent a fax to the mysterious Bilderberg office at Leiden in Holland on 7 April 2009 asking if I might attend the conference as an observer and whether some interviews could be arranged for me, for example with David Rockefeller or Henry Kissinger. One would have assumed this to be normal procedure at any conference, but I was mistaken. I received a fax the very next day with the unsympathetic reply:

Dated 8 April 2009, it said: 'Dear Herr Wisnewski, Regarding your phone-call and fax message of yesterday I confirm herewith that you will be sent a press announcement and a list of participants as soon as these are published. Regarding your other questions I confirm that attendance is by invitation only, and I am not in a position to arrange interviews for you as you have requested. Sincerely: M. B., Head Secretary.'

I was thus obliged to make use of alternative sources of information. On the internet the conference location was given as the Hotel Nafsika Astir Palace at Vouliagmeni near Athens. But I was suspicious of this since Vouliagmeni had been intended for the 2008 meeting before it was moved to the USA at the last moment. So I decided to phone the American journalist Jim Tucker who has been tracking the Bilderbergers for decades. Tucker counts as the grand old man among the tiny group of Bilderberg critics. A call to *American Free Press*, the self-styled 'maverick' weekly paper for which he works, yields his personal number. I can barely understand Tucker's gravelly American voice over the phone. But I gather nevertheless that the summit is indeed intended to take place this year at Vouliagmeni near Athens from 14 to 17 May. How is he so sure, I ask. 'Inside info', he grunts. Is he going himself? 'Yes' is his reply.

For me this is the starting-signal for booking my flight and a hotel. Early in April 2009 I search a map on the internet for a hotel in the vicinity of the Nafsika Astir Palace. And I find one. The Plaza Vouliagmeni Strand Hotel appears to be only about a kilometre away. A week before the conference I call *American Free Press* again, for confirmation that those chaps are indeed intending to fly over. The woman at the desk puts me through to someone called Bernie Davids. Another gravelly American voice, though somewhat stronger. I discover that the Americans have booked at the same hotel. Since I'll be flying alone I tell Bernie my travel details. If I fail to show up at the Plaza Vouliagmeni by midnight on 12 May 2009, please would he make enquiries. It has, after all, happened before now that a colleague on his way to the Bilderbergers was held up at the airport. 'Don't worry', says Bernie cheerfully, 'we'll meet at the bar. Just look out for three sozzled Americans!'

I was happy to proceed as suggested. In fact there were no problems or delays at Athens airport, which is surprising considering that dozens of VIPs would soon be arriving – the equivalent, perhaps, of 120 'state visits'. Arriving safely at the reception desk a week later I hear Bernie's gravelly voice in the distance: 'Is that our German friend?!' 'Are you already drunk?' I ask in reply to his joke over the phone. 'We're working on it!' he calls back. Welcome to the strange world of the Bilderberg hunters.

## 13.5.09: *In the globalist paradise*

Athens, 15 April 447 BC. Strange goings on in a temple. Some distance apart lie two large piles of potsherds. Citizens enter dressed in their light, flowing robes, take a potsherd from one, write something on it and then place it on the other. Those who are unable to write carry their potsherd to a corner where someone else scribbles on it. Soon a variety of names (for example 'Pericles', 'Cimon', or 'Aristeides') have been inscribed, and the pile is growing ever larger.

This is what is known as an *ostrakophoria*, from Greek *ostrakon* – potsherd. Citizens wrote the names of unpopular Athenians on pieces of pottery. If a name occurred six thousand times or more, the citizen in question had to leave Athens for ten years. Today some believe that Athenians were able by this method to banish contemporaries who were considered too powerful.

13 May 2009. The days of that popular method of voting by potsherd are long gone. Nowadays the powerful rule by whatever means they like.

This amounts to saying that something is wrong in that pretty bay of Vouliagmeni. While carefree teenagers splash about happily on the beach, one police car after another rushes by on the embankment road as though someone has stirred up a hornets' nest. And by following the rush in a taxi one arrives at the Nafsika Astir Palace hotel complex which is situated above the spot where the coastal road ends.

Whereas the 'death strip' dividing Germany has long since disappeared, a new such strip has been set up along, of all places, this idyllic Greek coastline. At the entrance to the Nafsika Astir Palace one finds oneself staring down the barrels of machine guns and at bullet-proof vests. The taxi is immediately surrounded by two or three security men with mirrors on wheels which they use to inspect its underside in detail. As of today the Nafsika Astir Palace is off limits for the global proletariat. Not even a mouse will be let in unless its name is on the list, so for us, too, there is nothing for it but to turn back.

Only the best is good enough for the Bilderbergers: In its adverts for tourists the Nafsika Astir Palace is described as being a 'magical paradise' among pine-trees in a unique natural setting, and as having breathtaking views of the Saronic Gulf. Viewed from the sea, however, it looks like an insect nest made of honeycomb-shaped concrete caves.

Yet the actual hornets haven't even arrived yet. Officially the Bilderberg Conference begins tomorrow, 14 May 2009. But the precaution has been taken of sealing off the location at least one day in advance. The whole of the Vouliagmeni peninsula is in quarantine. The Litous Street / Apollonos Street crossing is closed. Black-clad, heavily-armed police stand menacingly on the kerb. Uniformed guards shout at passing cars and gesticulate wildly. Clusters of stand-to police lean out of inconspicuous white vans. Passers-by are questioned by civilian snoopers: Who are you, what are you doing here, are you a journalist? The few journalists who intend to inform the population of Greece, and indeed of the world, about all the strange goings-on are spied on, arrested and searched.

This would be a very good time for a new *ostrakophoria*. Up on the small peninsula's hill, in the Nafsika Astir Palace, there are 130 personages who would most certainly deserve to have their names written on potsherds. Beginning with Prince Philippe of Belgium, bosses of the national banks of Greece, Belgium, Italy and Holland, European Central Bank boss Jean-Claude Trichet, and on to the President of the World Bank, the General Seretary of NATO, and many ministers from many European countries, right up to government chiefs such as Werner Faymann from Austria, Matti Vanhanen from Finland and German Minister-Presidents such as Roland Koch. In addition the bosses of world conglomerates such as Coca-Cola, Axa and Royal Dutch Shell, together with political strategists and media people (such as Matthias Nass of *Die Zeit*). Whereas the Greeks of old knew exactly who held the power in their state, today's local population don't even realize that their peaceful peninsula has been transformed into the navel of the world for four days.

However meagre the information regarding the Bilderberg Conference may be on this first day, there is one rule of thumb which is obvious already. The size of the media presence stands in opposite proportion to the significance of an international meeting: the greater the importance of the meeting, the smaller the number of journalists. The guiding maxim of our supposed 'information society' is: the smaller the publicity, the greater the importance. While hundreds of journalists disport themselves around G8 Summits consisting of a handful of globalists, there will be a mere handful of reporters gathering here for a meeting of hundreds of globalists. Those who are familiar with the media circus surrounding the G8 conferences would not believe that the elephantine circle of over one hundred Bilderberg strategists is being watched by a mere half dozen journalists – for whom, moreover, there is not a red carpet in sight.

The 'Press Centre' in the neighbouring Plaza Vouliagmeni is easily scanned, consisting as it does of a few reserved seats in the hotel lobby. In addition to Jim Tucker and his friends from *American Free Press*, the new arrivals are Paul Dorneanu and a colleague from Romania, Giorgio Bombassei from Belgium, Sybille van Steenberghe from France, bloggers Christoph Klöppner and Salam Mahdi, and myself.

### 14.5.09: The hunt for Rockefeller's swimming trunks

By ten in the morning the sun is already very hot. Waiting for a taxi with Salam Mahdi from Germany and Bernie Davids and Peter Papaheraklis from the USA, I quickly abandon my plan of renting a quiet domicile where I might write. It's only mid-May, so in June, July and August the heat in Athens and surroundings will be unbearable.

Taxis here are known as 'cabs' and they are the same bright yellow as their New York cousins. We get in and set off. Our aim is to find a marina near Athens where we can hire a boat from which to observe the Bilderbergers' hotel bunker and perhaps even catch one or two of the mighty ones on camera. The hotel is situated on a hill sloping westwards down to the sea, so that it can only be viewed properly from the water.

But this plan grows ever more complicated as we drive back and forth among forests of masts in the yachting bay. Smart motor yachts cost 1200 euros per day, but this is more than we want to invest in a possible snap of David Rockefeller in his swimming trunks. After a two-hour search we happen to meet Antonis high up near Piraeus, one of Greece's largest yachting marinas. He's sitting by the water on some dumped furniture under a tattered sun umbrella. At first glance he doesn't look particularly trustworthy in his ragged clothes. His long, greying yellow hair hangs down his back in a pony tail and is crowned with a baseball cap. A small red T-shirt is tight across his stout belly. As Peter Papaheraklis is originally from Greece he takes over the negotiations. After about half an hour we reach agreement with Antonis: 160 euros per day for the boat plus 140 for Antonis. Although Bernie has numerous sailing qualifications, he would have to cope with the unfamiliar boat in unfamiliar surroundings, while Antonis can get us to our destination as easily as a trip by car to the nearest market.

*The Nafsika Astir Palace is situated on a hill sloping westwards down to the sea, so that it can only be viewed properly from the water*

Apropos: We buy water, beer, some sandwiches and chocolate in a supermarket and then set off. The yacht is moored with its stern to the quay. Let's hope this trip along a narrow plank will remain the most dangerous part of today's expedition. We stuff our purchases into the boat's fridge and then Antonis skilfully sets off. It's a nice boat, about ten metres long, with a folding canopy over the cockpit. Surely I could sail this thing by myself? But of course we're not intending to do any sailing today – much too bothersome. Instead, Antonis keeps the diesel motor chugging, even once we've left the harbour. It's a perfect day. The bow splashes quietly through the water and the boat rocks gently. All the while, the lightly ruffled surface of the blue sea, the sunshine and the yacht threaten to undermine my work ethic. Repeatedly I do battle with myself against laying the camera aside and simply settling down comfortably on deck.

But of course we're supposed to be getting on with something. Antonis chugs along, parallel with the coastline and making straight for Vouliagmeni. After about three quarters of an hour, perhaps three nautical miles from our objective, we receive the first tactful

*A friendly tip from the Greek navy: You can't go beyond this point*

hint. A Greek navy dinghy suddenly appears, apparently from nowhere. These boats travel very fast and because of the noise your own boat makes you hardly hear them approaching. Gesticulating, the dark-clad crew call out to Antonis.

Then the dinghy slopes away from us and rushes off after another sailing boat. But since there's no need to react immediately to every official hint, we carry on towards Vouliagmeni and the Nafsika Astir Palace. Another quarter of an hour passes and we begin to realize that a snap of Rockefeller in his swimming trunks probably won't materialize. Threatening silhouettes of warships suddenly begin to appear in the distant haze. Quietly and seemingly immobile their hulls sit there in front of the Vouliagmeni peninsula like grey sharks. Behind them Josef Ackermann, Roland Koch and Siemens director Peter Lösching are having lunch with 124 other captains of finance and industry from all over Europe and especially from the USA. That is, according to the list of participants. And the secret services are at the table with them.

Through our zoom lenses we make out immobile figures on the bridge of one of the grey navy ships. There is no doubt that they can also see us. And sure enough: as the grey hulls slowly come closer we receive a further visit from 'our' dinghy. In an obviously threatening gesture it rushes up and circles round us. A shouted conversation takes place between its crew and Antonis. And then it disappears once more. Antonis mumbles that we're not allowed to go any further. But the Bilderberg look-outs appear unconvinced by his change of course. A larger speedboat from the Greek coast-guards rushes up, hooting loudly. 'No cameras!' they bellow. They're serious this time, it seems. I disappear below deck with the camera, remove the memory card and hide it. My top priority is to save the pictures. Over the coming days, this attitude proves to be highly appropriate.

Wanting neither to get ourselves arrested nor to saddle Antonis with a hefty fine, we have no alternative but to turn back. We give in. We couldn't get closer than two miles to the Bilderber-

*Navy and coastguard in front of the Bilderbergers' hotel*

gers' hotel. To help us relax, Antonis chugs to a bay near a former Greek prison island now inhabited solely by seagulls. With our anchor down, and still somewhat shocked by the warlike array, we at last permit ourselves a beer. We agree that for a summit that is not supposed to be taking place the security measures are quite something.

### 15.5.09: No Plan B at the checkpoint

The nerves of the Greek policemen at the crossing in front of the Bilderbergers' hotel at Vouliagmeni are on edge. It's a question of when, not whether, heads will roll. For days they've been inspecting every car aiming for the coast road towards the Nafsika Astir Palace, and now this. Eight large coaches full of communist demonstrators have just sailed past them and are preparing to stop in front of the hotel in order to discharge their noisy passengers there. How this could have happened isn't yet clear; but it certainly wasn't planned or authorized.

*The crossing in front of the Nafsika Astir Palace*

*Civilian vans carrying police*

This is made obvious by the way the duped officers now shout at every small car that annoys them. It's too late; the coaches have got through. The policemen bellow, whistle and gesticulate wildly. The power of the state is losing its nerve. That accidents are avoided is entirely down to the circumspection of the car drivers. One driver, however, stops his vehicle in the middle of the crossing and makes to continue up the coastal road on foot. 'Arrest me, then!' he shouts when the men blow their whistles. And with his arms crossed on his chest he plants himself in front of several black-clad anti-terror officers.

But there is no reaction. Unlike ordinary policemen on the beat, they are trained to cope with the racket of battle as horses are trained to tolerate the thunder of cannon. Externally, the power of the state, clad in the latest fashion of anti-terror gear, stands there calm and composed. But inwardly they must be fuming at this bitter defeat. It seems that at this crossing the police are prepared to deal solely with housewives, commuters and tourists in their cars. Faced with someone who merely wants to drive across, they evidently have no Plan B. In fact, this operation demonstrates the impotence of the state's power. For in the vicinity of the conference which is not supposed to be taking place, there can surely be no question of shooting at coaches carrying civilians.

Unlike scattered demonstrators and small groups who tend to look on helplessly as the global negative elites get on with their machinations, communists demonstrate with all their might, as one

*Demo-coaches in front of the Bilderbergers' hotel at Vouliagmeni near Athens in 2009*

can if one has a plan and knows what one wants to achieve, and also when one has detailed knowledge of the location.

While it's all going on I creep past the helpless police in order to watch the demo in front of the Bilderbergers' hotel. The communists have taken up position in the driveway almost in military formation and are abusing the Bilderbergers in unison with all their might. I almost faint when I realize that after a rather uneventful day I've left my camera behind in my room. Daylight is beginning to fade. On the spur of the moment I refigure my mobile phone into a journalistic all-round weapon and photograph the demo. Then I move closer to the cheer-leader and send a report to the internet blog 'Schall und Rauch' [Smoke and Mirrors].[3] As soon as I've made contact with Fred Mann of 'Schall und Rauch' I hold up the mobile and signal to the cheer-leader that I'm ready:

'IMPERIALISTS, GET OUT OF GREECE', he bellows into his microphone, and now also into my mobile. And the crowd replies:

'SOCIALISM IS THE FUTURE OF THE WORLD' – 'CAPITALISM

*Entrance to the Bilderbergers' hotel near Athens in 2009*

IS ROTTEN AND DYING' – 'THE GREEK COMMUNIST PARTY IS STRONG – GET READY TO ATTACK'

It's a long time since we heard choruses like this at home in Germany. 'Divine!!!' a user later writes in the blog. 'Wow. That's encouraging!' says another.

A slightly shortened version of my report to Fred Mann at 'Schall und Rauch':

*Mann*: How many protesters are there?

*Wisnewski*: About 200 to 300. It's the Greek Communist Party. This is a terrific coup for them. They drove right up to the Bilderbergers' hotel in more than half a dozen coaches. Even though the street below was closed to traffic. We don't yet know why they were let through. Whatever the case may be, it was super cheeky or super bold, whichever way you look at it. They're thoroughly organized and are putting on a huge demo right in front of the Bilderbergers' entrance. There are lots of police in the background. They are extremely nervous, shouting at anyone who mistakenly tries to pass

*The hotel entrance during the demo (with cheer-leader)*

*The cheer-leader in front of the Bilderbergers' hotel at Vouliagmeni*

*Professional demo culture in front of the Bilderbergers' hotel at Vouliagmeni*

by car. It's come close to fights between car drivers and the police. They're definitely hyper-nervous and have obviously lost control. We really weren't expecting anything else to happen. But this party is totally organized. They've planned this attack with military precision.

*Mann:* So do the Greeks realize what's happening?

*Wisnewski:* There are no other protesters here. This is evidently an exclusive operation by the Greek Communist Party. Apart from this demo, the whole thing is totally unnoticed by the population. I don't believe anyone knows what's really going on, what big shots are here. About 100 to 120 participants. We're not sure yet.

*Mann:* Have you seen any of the big shots yet?

*Wisnewski:* No. It's impossible. So far as we know they came through this little place secretly in the middle of the night. These Bilderbergers have certainly learnt a thing or two ... The police are now marching up towards the demonstration ...

*Mann:* Are you in the midst of it or watching from the sidelines?

*Wisnewski:* I'm about twenty or thirty metres away. You can certainly say now that the Bilderbergers won't find it so easy to get away with this any longer. It used to be something no-one knew anything about. But now, wherever it happens, there seems to be one group or another that's ready to step forward and organize a protest.

*Mann:* It's a good thing for them to notice that they can't be incognito any longer.

*Wisnewski:* I agree. These Bilderbergers have done all kinds of things to make themselves disappear into a kind of black hole of anonymity. But now things are beginning to go a bit wrong despite the conference hotel being so out of the away, even in relation to this small village of Vouliagmeni near Athens. The population hardly notices anything.

(Demo choruses)

*Mann:* How d'you think the situation is going to develop?

*Wisnewski:* No idea. The police have now formed up again in the background. At this moment it looks as though no-one has any idea about what to do next ... Wait a moment, please.

Yes, they appear to be getting ready to march forward ... I've no idea what they're going to do.

(Demo choruses)

*Mann*: Are they carrying placards or anything?

*Wisnewski*: Yes. Lots of red flags. 'Communist Party of Greece' seems to be written on them. Stupidly I can't read the Greek script. And there are large placards. Wait a moment. I'm now going up close to the front of the demo. Here's the cheer-leader, and behind him are the police ... Just a second.

*Mann*: Can you ask him anything?

*Wisnewski and the cheer-leader (speaking in English)*:

*Wisnewski*: What do they [the police] want to do now?

*Cheer-leader*: They're just watching. But I'm not sure. Perhaps they want to scare us, to terrorize us.

*Wisnewski*: But you're not intending to force your way in, are you?

*Cheer-leader*: No, we're not aggressive.

*Wisnewski*: I believe you. This operation by the police seems to me to be meaningless.

*Cheer-leader*: There's a meaning in everything; especially here. What they mean to do is terrorize us. They're trying to frighten us. But we're fighting for our rights.

*Wisnewski*: Does it make you scared when you see all this?

*Cheer-leader*: No. One thing's certain, and that is that we're not scared.

*Fred Mann asks Wisnewski*: How many police d'you think there are?

*Wisnewski*: I should say about forty or fifty. But that's surely only the vanguard. If I look a bit further along the street, toward the hotel, there are sure to be many more over there. They'll be staggered somewhat. I expect the police are raising the temperature a bit, but I don't think they'll succeed.

(Demo choruses)

THE END

*Richard Toibin is arrested near the 2009 Bilderberg Conference at Vouliagmeni near Athens*

As quickly as they arrived, the communists return to their coaches. Twilight is coming on, and we suddenly feel very isolated here in front of the Bilderbergers' hotel. We're afraid they'll seize our photos and videos and so we, too, take to our heels in a hurry.

### 16.5.09: The transparent hornets' nest of the Bilderbergers

The Vouliagmeni police station is a low, white building. The site is surrounded by a green metal fence, and a policeman with a pistol is on guard at the entrance. Inside are two dozen patrol police, reserve police, secret service officers and security personnel. And our friend Richard Toibin from Ireland. And that's the problem.

Richard has come to Vouliagmeni from Ireland with his girlfriend because he's interested in the Bilderberg phenomenon. And this is his second arrest – during a further demonstration, this time by Greek nationalists. As a reaction to yesterday's embarrassment with the communists, the police cordon has been moved by at least an additional kilometre back into the village. And this time, as well as the parked police vehicles, the streets have been cordoned off with police tape. And a troop of police reservists is also at the ready.

The trouble is that Richard appears to be no closer to leaving the police station. My colleague Giorgio Bombassei from Brussels and I are wondering what to do. Should I go into the police station with a microphone attached to my shirt collar and linked to his camera, while he covers the entrance from the other side of the street? We reject this idea, however, and assume that it would be better to go in 'unarmed'. A 'listening attack' might act as a provocation. So I remove the transmitter from the inside pocket of my jacket and take the tiny microphone off my shirt collar. Instead I get out my press card and walk slowly down the street holding it up in my right hand. I address the officer with the machine pistol with a friendly 'Hi'. 'Does anyone speak English?' I ask. After a moment's consideration he nods and opens the squeaky gate. Very calmly I walk up the half dozen steps to the entrance. The door is open because the place is as busy as a dovecote. Inside I find totally stressed faces. It's very hot and some of the officers are sweating profusely. 'Is that your press card?' one of them asks. 'Yes', I reply, while extending my hand instead of passing over the card. I smile. Smiles are what is needed, building confidence, treating people as human beings and, above all, as individuals. That's what is important. I make myself appear utterly amicable.

The police station is like a nest of agitated hornets; although surely no-one wants them to begin stinging. Slowly, still holding up my press card, I walk along the corridor, glancing casually into the different rooms. Nervous discussions everywhere, and sweaty faces. Every version of Greek police uniform is here: from the blue mix of the regular police patrols and on to the navy blue or black of reservists and anti-terror squads resembling those of German GSG 9 counter-terrorism units. Among these are also security guys elegantly clad in black. Probably the secret service.

Yet very little here is secret at the moment, least of all that modest little coffee-party of over one hundred global leading figures up at the Nafsika Astir Palace luxury hotel.

The mood at the police station is uncomfortable. After all, a good deal has gone amiss over the past few days. As their hysterical reactions showed, the officers had been caught very much on the hop by recent events. The fact that today's demo of Greek nationalists came up against cordoned off streets over a kilometre further out than yesterday's checkpoint shows that the communists' demo had amounted to a serious failure of the police.

I find Richard in the farthest room at the end of the corridor. He is seated by the window with his back to the balcony. There's a desk at right-angles to him with police officers crowded round it. In my friendliest manner I say that I've just popped in to see how Richard is getting on. He is somewhat shocked and keeps rubbing his hands. We're allowed to talk briefly. I ask what happened. He says he'd taken a photo of some policemen and had consequently been arrested. I ask the police spokesman what Richard is accused of. He says he took photos of the police; on being questioned he had no identity card to show them. So that's why they've brought him here. After all, they don't know who he is. And it's forbidden to take pictures of police personnel.

Except for the shocked expression on his face he seems to be alright. I approach the spokesman again. I tell him I also took photos of the police during the demo just now. The man in the blue uniform is not pleased to hear this. They were only doing their job, he parries. There is obviously no proper means by which to justify arresting someone for photographing the police. I counter that I, too, am merely doing my job. Oh, yes, he warns me. And then he begins to shout in English: 'Get out! Get out!' He's obviously in a very bad mood. 'I, too, shall be doing my job,' I say again, glancing at Richard. More clearly expressed threats are not going to be much use at the moment. 'Watch out,' I say to Richard. And then I leave the room and dawdle back down the passage as slowly as I came.

Our colleagues are waiting on the opposite side of the street. They have filmed the goings on as best they could.

Soon Richard's girlfriend arrives with his ID. And then he's free to go. But he's had a bad shock. He'd been hearing the officers putting Greek 'inmates' through the mill and shouting at them. And he kept hearing the word 'Bilderberg'. And all the while our mobile phone conversations had been audible from some sort of loudspeakers. The police had evidently been listening to us all day long in this transparent building.

The nationalists' demo is over. And we return seemingly undetected to our hotel. In the event, everything is possible, from pinpointing our mobile conversations to the nearest metre while also recording every talk and every text message.

## 17.5.09: Writing and thinking undesirable – a pleasant chat by the wayside

17 May 2009: Today we intend to have a really good rest at the Vouliagmeni Oceanis: that marvellous terrace above the ocean, the cool breeze from the sea and the excellent food. The end of the Bilderberg Conference is approaching. No more chasing after black limousines and playing hide-and-seek with the police. As my German blogger friends Salam and Christoph set off in the direction of the hotel I decide to permit myself another beer. No sooner said than done. But suddenly my mobile rings. It's my Romanian friend, journalist Paul Dorneanu. He's just arrived back at the hotel after being interrogated together with all the other arrested journalists. I'd better come straight away.

I'm immediately sober and promise to be as quick as I can. I pay and leave the hotel by the exit to the street. I'm about to go to the crossing leading to the hotel when I sober up even more. I see two policemen there, pointing towards me. We have in the meantime become very well acquainted with at least some of the officers.

Fortunately the Oceanis terrace has two entrances, so I can immediately disappear back into the next one. I then switch off my mobile and shut myself in the toilet for half an hour. When nothing happens, I leave the Oceanis again, this time through the main entrance, passing a black-clad reserve policeman who doesn't react.

My endeavour to reach my hotel via another route then leads to the encounter with the Greek secret policewoman and her sporty partner, described at the beginning of this book. By means of her questions she shows me, unequivocally, that writing and thinking are not desirable in connection with the Bilderberg Conference; so in order to avoid any more bother I abruptly break off the conversation with her by saying 'Nice to have met you', and go on my way.

There's no march-past and no band playing as the Bilderbergers take their leave of Vouliagmeni. A sure sign they've gone: all the police and look-outs have vanished. The state of emergency is over. The Litous Street / Apollonos Street junction is open again as though nothing has ever happened. The Bilderbergers' ghostly conference is over – until the same time next year at a new location.

*The arrested journalists at the Plaza Vouliagmeni after their release on 17 May 2009*

Although governments, states and unions may come and go, the Bilderbergers go on forever as they labour on at building the world of tomorrow. Whether we like it or not is irrelevant; the days of the *ostrakophoria* came to an end two and a half thousand years ago.


## 19.5.09: A fax from Leiden

So what is the outcome of my three 'trips to the Bilderbergers' at Rottach-Egern, Oosterbeek and Vouliagmeni? The phantom conference really does exist. But in contrast to the G8 Summit it is not at all public; in fact, it is kept as far as possible out of the public eye. Even the locals are virtually unaware of the global might's presence in their vicinity. While the conference is in progress the surroundings teem with guards in uniform, but even more with civilian police, secret service personnel and security details who are not in uniform. And then the Bilderbergers depart again as unobtrusively as they arrived. But why? What is it that has to be kept hidden? Why are the government bosses attending a G8 Summit made to dance like circus horses while those others prefer to stay out of the limelight?

On my return to Munich I hear that the Bilderberg Conference is the only meeting which announces itself after the event, although in the future tense: 'The Bilderberg Conference will take place from 14 to 17 May 2009 at Vouliagmeni, Greece', says the official press notice dated 17 May 2009. Perhaps some people did receive this fax 'already' on 17 May, but I didn't get it till 19 May. The official fax of the 'Bilderberg Conference' confirms: The conference will be held in Vouliagmeni, Greece, 14–17 May 2009.

The official press release is very general and non-committal:

> The conference will deal mainly with the financial crisis, government and markets, role of institutions, market economies and democracies, Iraq, Pakistan and Afghanistan, US and

the world, cyber-terrorism, new imperialisms, protectionism, post-Kyoto challenges.

Two thirds of the attendees were said to be from Europe and 'the remainder' from the USA. A significant euphemism. What it should really say is: One third of the attendees will be from the USA and the remainder from Europe. The most prominent quota of individuals is from the USA, and it is they, with Rockefeller, Wolfowitz and Perle, who will set the tone. Only one is absent from the list this time: geostrategist Henry Kissinger.

Studying the list, it's difficult to believe how many international politicians and business giants stole through Vouliagmeni, that small suburb of Athens, in order to meet in utter secrecy at the Nafsika Astir Palace. But the document that comes buzzing out of my fax machine on 19 May 2009 leaves one in no doubt. To the top of the hill on that small peninsula near Athens came Josef Ackermann with US National Security Agency (NSA) Director Keith Alexander, former Siemens Director Klaus Kleinfeld and present CEO Peter Löscher with NATO Secretary General Jaap de Hoop Scheffer, Minister-President of Hesse Roland Koch with H. R. H. Prince Philippe, President of Airbus S.A.S. CEO Thomas Enders with National Bank of Greece Chairman and CEO Takis Arapoglou, the Foreign Policy Spokesman of Germany's CDU/CSU, Eckart von Klaeden with Austrian Federal Chancellor Werner Faymann, and Swiss publisher Michael Ringier with US tycoon David Rockefeller.

And many others were present as well. The list contains 127 names, from A for Ackermann to Z for Zoellick, President of the World Bank (see Appendix). Ministers, Prime Ministers and Federal Chancellors from all over Europe shook hands with bankers, finance sharks and American geostrategists. Also in attendance were numerous, in some cases notorious, figures in world politics such as former World Bank CEO James Wolfensohn, Swiss politician Christoph Blocher, ultra-right US foreign policy 'Prince of Darkness' Richard Perle, and Jean-Claude Trichet, President of the

European Central Bank. Add to this the fact that the list is not necessarily complete. In the past one has often heard of guests at the conference who were not officially listed. For example you could search the 2008 list in vain for the name of Barack Obama. Yet he is said to have been there.

# The collective might of the Bilderbergers

What's in a name? Of course we know Helmut Kohl, Angela Merkel, Peter Mandelson. But what about Richard Dearlove or John Kerr? Sure, they're prominent people, but so what! However spectacular some individual names may be, the endless Bilderberg lists as a whole don't really add up to much. Moreover, while the names of the participants may have something to tell us, the names of the firms or institutions they represent are equally important.

In order to reach a better understanding of all this I have entered the participants since 1991 in a database. Although this only covers one third of Bilderberg history, my database already contains 2,300 entries, one for each position on a list, so that some personages appear several times. For example Josef Ackermann, who was Germany's most powerful banker. A search for 'Ackermann' yields five hits. We see that this Swiss manager attended the 1995 Bilderberg Conference when he was still CEO of Credit Suisse. There he was able to meet Hilmar Kopper, the strong man of Deutsche Bank. Ackermann didn't join the Board of Deutsche Bank until 1996. In 2002 he became spokesman for the Board and in 2006 he was made Chairman of the Board. (Today, inter alia, he is on the Board of Directors of Royal Dutch Shell.) Well, five entries in 18 years are not all that many. But we see a very different picture when we search the database for Deutsche Bank. All of a sudden there's a hailstorm of 27 hits. Deutsche Bank has been represented annually since 1991 by at least one heavyweight. Besides Ackermann there have been long-time Board Spokesman (from 1989 till 1997) and Board Director Hilmar Kopper and Director Ulrich Cartellieri.

## Example: Deutsche Bank

So to make really clear to ourselves the powerful influences that have been coming together on the hill of Vouliagmeni and in many other locations for over fifty years, it is not enough to look only at participants' names. What we also need are the names of the institutions and companies they represent. From this we can then gather that the Bilderbergers represent billions, which makes them one of the mightiest clubs ever known on earth.

Deutsche Bank, for example, amounting in 2009 to a 127th of Bilderberg Conference participants, had in 2008 a balance of two billion euros and was the central financial turnover point of the German economy. And while banks give credits and acquire shares, they also frequently sit on the boards of large enterprises.

'More than for their financial power, large banks are criticized for the influence they exercise through shareholdings, proxy voting powers and seats on boards of directors', writes Hans-Jürgen Albers in the standard work *Handbuch zur ökonomischen Bildung* (a business studies textbook):

> Banks own shares in the capital of numerous industrial and commercial firms. Thus, for example, Deutsche Bank possesses share packages in DaimlerChrysler and Karstadt. Even more significant is the power banks exercise through proxy voting rights. According to #135 AktG, a bank must be instructed by a vote of the general meeting, but most proxy customers follow the bank's advice. On account of the proxy voting powers, banks have a far greater influence than would be due to them on the basis of their shareholdings.[4]

Deutsche Bank has countless seats on boards of directors (currently more than four hundred) and thus far-reaching influence. For example Deutsche Bank Director Dr Clemens Börsig has or had a seat on the board of directors of Deutsche Lufthansa AG (until April 2008), Linde AG, Heidelberger Druckmaschinen AG (until March

2007), Bayer AG (since April 2007), and Daimler AG (since April 2007). Deputy Chairman Dr Karl-Gerhard Eick is or was on the board of directors of DeTe Immobilien, Deutsche Telekom Immobilien und Service GmbH, T-Mobile International AG, T-Systems Enterprise Services GmbH, T-Systems Business Services GmbH, FC Bayern München AG, and Corpus Immobiliengruppe GmbH & Co KG (since September 2007).

And there is even more to the power of banks and especially of Deutsche Bank:

> By being a company's bank and having seats on its board of directors, a bank has access to internal information about the enterprise which can provide insider advantages over other investors on the capital market.[5]

German banks hear, see and know everything and can have their say everywhere. Deutsche Bank, however, is number one. The Federal Government may or may not govern Germany. But Deutsche Bank, the almost omnipotent spider in the web of the German economy, certainly plays its part in the job. It has shares in giant concerns such as Axel Springer and Daimler, of which the directors also participate regularly in the Bilderberg Conferences. CEO Ackermann sits or has sat, inter alia, on the boards of Bayer AG and Siemens AG, which in their turn have also been represented at Bilderberg Conferences by leading figures such as Gerhard Cromme, Peter Löscher, Klaus Kleinfeld and Ulrich Cartellieri.

Deutsche Bank is the sun of the German economy, around which (almost) everything rotates. When a representative of Deutsche Bank sits down on a chair, it had better be standing on firm ground in order to bear his weight. Yet Deutsche Bank only occupies one or two of the 100 or 150 seats at those shadowy Bilderberg Conferences. Weighing billions, it is joined – often regularly – by other German conglomerates weighing milliards. Apart from those mentioned above, the list contains Linde AG, Hochtief AG, ThyssenKrupp AG, Deutsche Post AG, Airbus, Burda, Herrenknecht

AG, BASF and others. And these are joined by influential politicians such as Angela Merkel, Guido Westerwelle, Eckart von Klaeden, Eberhard Sandschneider (German Society for Foreign Policy), Friedbert Pflüger, Ruprecht Polenz, Karl A. Lamers among many more.

Apart from Ackermann, the 2009 conference was attended by persons with positions in or connections with the following enterprises: Goldman Sachs, American International Group (AIG), Citigroup, Bayer, Alcoa, Ford, Gillette, McDonald's, Dow Jones, American Express, MetLife, Fannie Mae, EADS, Lazard Frères, Microsoft, Nokia, Shell, BP, Sandoz, Pepsi, Novartis, Delta, PayPal, Facebook, Kohlberg Kravis Roberts, General Dynamics, Telecom Italia, IMPRESA, Fit, Coca-Cola, EXOR, ING Group, Akzo Nobel and Investor AB.

There were also numerous national banks such as US Federal Reserve, Banca d'Italia, Nederlandsche Bank, and in addition ministers, professors and global organizations like NATO (represented by its General Secretary), the European Central Bank and the World Bank.

In short: Sitting together with the Bilderbergers you'll find a large part of the financial, commercial and military powers of the planet, including the secret services. The latter are frequently present including, for example in 2009, Keith D. Alexander, boss of the notorious American secret service NSA (National Security Agency). The NSA is the planet's Big Brother, spying on everything and everybody. All forms of electronic communication, whether internet, e-mail, fax or telephone, are targeted and listened to by NSA.

The power concentrated around a Bilderberg Conference is in the truest sense of the word totalitarian. A secret regime, of which the individual members dominate whole economies and states, meets annually and in private. Should this not make us wonder what's going on? How and why did the group come into existence in the first place?

# Part 2

# THE SECRET BACKGROUND

# A conspirator founds the Bilderbergers

Thick fog surrounds us on all sides when we search for an answer to the question at the end of the last chapter. Even the few good books that have so far been written about the Bilderbergers have not entirely solved the mystery of their origins and background. Daniel Estulin, for instance, says that Prince Bernhard of the Netherlands (the first 'president' of the Bilderbergers) had adopted the belief that 'far-reaching disasters, such as the economic collapse of the 1920s, could be avoided if responsibly-minded, influential leaders would quietly take charge of world affairs themelves.'[6] In other words, the totalitarian early-Platonic idea of leadership by the elite in which the Bilderbergers would rule as a dictatorship of philosophers over western democracies. This may well be partly true, but it lacks a very essential component, and in Estulin's book that missing component goes by the name of 'one'.

It is said that 'one' approached Prince Bernhard with the request 'that he organize an initial gathering of "like-minded" representatives from all over the world and from every field of commerce, politics, industry and the military at the Hotel De Bilderberg in Oosterbeek, Holland'.[7] So that is where 'one' gathered for a meeting between 29 and 31 May 1954, and where 'the founding members' elaborated their tasks and aims. But who was 'one'? Who was it who approached Prince Bernhard? And who, apart from Prince Bernhard, were 'the founding members'? There is nothing about this in Estulin's chapter on 'The Founding of the Bilderberg Club'.

Andreas von Rétyi comes a great deal closer to giving us an answer. He devoted a whole chapter to 'one', giving him the designation 'The Grey Eminence'. And he names him as Joseph Hieronim Retinger, of whom I had never heard. The astonishing truth is that the international elephants' club of the Bilderbergers was indeed founded by a nobody.

## The most important characteristics of a monk

Who was Joseph Hieronim Retinger? We can be grateful to von Rétyi for referring in detail to the biography by Retinger's long-time secretary, John Pomian: *Memoirs of an Eminence Grise* (Sussex 1972). There we read about Retinger's time as a student at the Sorbonne in Paris (from 1906), and about who – among the Polish aristocrats – kept an eye on their compatriot there. He was awarded his doctorate aged just twenty. No longer a student, he founded a Polish office in London in 1911, whereupon he was immediately invited to an appointment with the Prime Minister. Moreover, he worked for the British Secret Service during World War II.

The founding father of the Bilderbergers working for the Secret Service? 'Retinger became ever more deeply involved in undercover, not to say Secret Service, activities', writes von Rétyi.[8] It is also interesting to note that for Retinger, founder of the Bilderbergers, there was nothing despicable about 'conspiracies' – quite the reverse, in fact. As a member of a nation under oppression during occupation by the Nazis, he felt that conspiracies were a citizen's primary duty: 'For western ears the word conspiracy has an ugly ring', von Rétyi quotes Retinger: 'But how different is its significance in Poland where a person would be ashamed if he were not a conspirator. National conspiracy was the expression used for the secret continuation of national life under enemy occupation. Almost from the very day when the government moved to Romania the conspiracy began which ultimately embraced the whole nation.' Retinger led an adventurous life during World War II. He parachuted behind enemy lines into his homeland Poland in order to supply the resistance movement there with cash. 'In this way

Retinger found himself in the midst of that dangerous morass of conspiracy, underground activities and secret services.'[9]

It goes without saying that we can sympathize with Retinger's commitment to his homeland; but the fact remains that the Bilderbergers hark back to a professional conspirator who was also a British agent. But this still does not entirely solve the mystery surrounding him, as von Rétyi remarks:

'He always appeared to keep himself in the background, playing a mysterious, rather obscure role throughout his life... He was taken – rightly – to be extremely influential', von Rétyi quotes Retinger's secretary Pomain, 'but no-one appeared to be in a position to give a short answer to the question as to why and to what extent this was the case. He never occupied an official post, never had much money, and never participated in public discussions.'[10]

'I remember Retinger once picking up the telephone in the United States and in no time at all having an appointment to meet the President', said a certain Sir Edward Beddington-Behrens in 1960 during his funeral oration for Retinger. 'And in Europe he had free access to every political circle – through a kind of right based on trust, devotion and loyalty.'[11] But how did Retinger acquire such influence? Why was it no problem for him to arrange a meeting with the President of the US or other high-standing personages? What was the power behind him? How far-reaching were his conspiracies really?

'Retinger was not among those who strove for wealth or power. He found himself in the highly unusual position of being acquainted with the rich and powerful without ever having possessed much himself... Genuinely valuable material goods left him cold... It was evident that all those things which made life worth living for other people had no value for Retinger.'[12] He did not even have a wife when he founded the Bilderbergers.

To sum up:

– The man had no possessions and cared nothing for money or material goods.

– He was neither married, nor is anything known about putative love affairs.
– The only known personal relationship he had was with his secretary, John Pomian.

No money, no possessions, no relationships. Perhaps we shall gain greater insight by using the words 'poverty' and 'chastity'. This would give us the most important characteristics of a monk. But surely monks live in monasteries, wear long habits and do not follow profane callings? Well, this may be true of most monks, but not of those discreet servants of the Society of Jesus, the 'Jesuits'.

In fact, Retinger did become a monk when he was a young man, and completed the novitiate of the Jesuits in Rome, as we are told by Jan Chciuk-Celt, a son of one of Retinger's fellow soldiers during the war. But as he found celibacy 'too great a hurdle' he gave up the priesthood. According to this report Retinger was actually married twice, first to a Polish woman called Otylia Zubrzycka and then, after parting from her, to a certain Stella Morel in 1926, 'daughter of his friend the Labour trade-unionist E.D. Morel'. (Chciuk-Celt, Jan: *Józef Hieronim Retinger 1888–1960*, updated 24 June 2009.) But after his second wife died in 1933 it seems that the widower Retinger never embarked on a new relationship but instead remembered his former Jesuit life and took up the labours of conspiracy.

It would be naïve to assume that powerful associations such as that of the Bilderbergers arose out of nothing, more than fifty-five years ago, on the basis of a few conversations. In reality the Bilderbergers are based on ancient structures to which they are giving a new outward form.

# The first globalists

It is the year 1521 and a knight is writhing in a feverish nightmare at the Basque castle of the Loyola family. After the Battle of Pamplona, French soldiers had found Inigo de Loyola (Ignatius Loyola) on the bastion of the citadel, 'covered in blood and with a shattered leg'. 'What a mockery that this daring knight should have been felled by such an impersonal weapon of war in those new modern times, a cannon ball arriving blindly from goodness knows where...'[13] Again and again during the subsequent months of agonizing pain and operations, Loyola was pursued by feverish fantasies and visions. Then, 'when the pain ceased to torment him, leaden hours of boredom plagued him'.[14] To alleviate his plight he went in search of his favourite book, which he had already read in his days as a page-boy, the Spanish romance *Amadis de Gaula* about the adventures of the legendary son of the King of Gaul and the English princess Elisena; he had been rejected as a baby and somehow made his way to Scotland where he fell in love with the enchanting Princess Oriana. However, the book was not to be found. The Loyola castle possessed precisely two works which dealt with quite another hero, namely Jesus Christ. These were four folios of the *Vita Christi* and also a collection of legends about the lives of the saints. And so brave young Inigo de Loyola transformed his life as a heroic knight into a life as a religious hero. He threw away his armour and exchanged it for a beggar's garb. He abandoned life as a knight and decided to become a fighter for Christ: 'One night he rose from his bed, knelt before the image of the Mother of God in the corner of the room and vowed to serve forthwith as a faithful soldier under the royal banner of Christ.'[15]

That just shows you where limited educational opportunities can lead! And so young Loyola put his vow into practice and founded, on 15 August 1534, a fan-club for his new hero, which in only a few years was calling itself the Society of Jesus (better known as the Jesuits) and which, in the parlance of the Church, was known as an 'Order'. On that day, in the chapel of St Denis on Montmartre, together with six other men, Loyola vowed to live in poverty, chastity and with a mission in Palestine.

If only the library of the Loyola castle had had a rather more varied stock of books, the world, so say critics of the Jesuits, would have been spared a great deal, inter alia the society of the Bilderbergers. Let us now turn our attention to the former in order to gain a rather better understanding of the latter.

### The Pope's fire-brigade

First of all, missionaries in those days were the first globalists, and the Jesuits were the topmost among those missionaries. To penetrate other cultures, to infiltrate them, to subvert them and turn them around in order to serve one's own purposes – that is what the Jesuits specialized in. When missionaries encountered especially hard nuts to crack in their missionary work, then the Pope called for his missionary fire-brigade, the Jesuits. For example in the 1630s the Christian church had a problem: it was proving difficult to make progress in Christianizing India. The cultural and religious barriers between Christian beliefs and the Indian religions appeared to be insurmountable. Especially the highest Hindu caste of the Brahmans was proving to be an impenetrable fortress. Brahmans were stamped with a very special elite identity developed over many centuries. It was an identity which had asserted itself within the Hindu caste system and had become especially resistant to outside influences. How would it be possible to penetrate this resistance in order to bring the 'glad tidings' of Jesus?

A number of Catholic orders had already been having a tough time of it: Dominicans, Franciscans and priests from all over the world had been spreading the Gospel in this new colonial region, but without any real success. In truth, the Brahmans especially found those stories of the Son of God pining away on the Cross very strange indeed. So King John III of Portugal decided to request the Pope to employ his new secret weapon, the Society of Jesus.

'The King had already heard much praise regarding the feats of those priests and hoped they would work with even greater zeal than the other missionaries to spread the word of God among the heathen. That decision of the King was indeed instrumental in bringing about an entirely new epoch for Catholic missionary work and also for the Society of Jesus. What the Jesuits achieved as preachers of the Gospel vastly overshadowed any successes other missionary orders may have had. And it was in fact this missionary work that brought world renown for the Society of Jesus.'[16]

The Jesuits revolutionized missionary style and thus also missionary success. Instead of acting aggressively they worked modestly, instead of making demands they made offers, instead of suppressing they gave advice and help, instead of boasting they showed humility, and instead of conflict they brought consensus – secretly and on the quiet, thus developing that typical 'Jesuit style'.

# Behind a thousand masks

And so the famous Francis Xavier, close friend of Loyola and the man of the hour, set off for India in order to crack the Hindu nut. He, too, had already learned 'how often one has to proceed with "saintly cunning" in order to achieve a pious goal', as Fülöp-Miller puts it.[17] 'So as soon as he arrived he treated the Hindu priests with the same clever obsequiousness usually practised by his teacher Ignatius in such situations.' But not only that. It was not solely the Brahman masters he treated in this way, but also, or indeed especially, their slaves! 'Especially for the downtrodden and maltreated slaves, those pious conversations with the missionary in many cases became the whole content of their further lives.'

And as a result:

> They helped him to the best of their ability in his endeavours and told him in secret about the lifestyle of their masters, how they behaved and what their vices and depravities were. In this way Xavier gained intimate knowledge of the character traits, interests and idiosyncrasies of the people he wanted to convert. Before even entering a house he knew whether he would be dealing with a man committing polygamy, or one who practised usury, or a person who was violent, or who shamelessly misused his office for purposes of extortion, or someone who mistreated his slaves. In carrying out his work of conversion by adhering to the teachings of his father Ignatius, Xavier became all things to all people.[18]

This was how the revolution in missionary work was brought about. Whereas other missionaries themselves frequently inflicted violence, oppression and diverse crimes on an indigenous population, the Jesuits proceeded in accordance with the motto: 'If it is your wish to achieve fruitful results in your soul and in the souls of others, you must always treat the sinners in a way that encourages them to trust you and open their hearts to you. These are living books that are more eloquent than dead books which you are otherwise obliged to study . . .' wrote Francis Xavier to his successor Gaspar Barzaeus.[19]

In short: The Jesuits revolutionized the relationship between action and reaction in missionary work. Whereas normally an action calls forth a reaction, the Jesuits developed a style which discouraged any opposition so that no reaction would come about. One can only defend oneself against something one can describe as being inimical. By unravelling that ancient dialectic the Jesuits made a new beginning. In almost every instance their actions were formulated in a way which did not give rise to inimical reactions. They developed what amounted to out-and-out secret-service methods and thus became one of the first well-organized secret services the world has known. Yes, they used agents as well as techniques of counterfeit and disguise:

> The Jesuit missionary Roberto de Nobili, nephew of Cardinal Bellarini and scion of an Italian family claiming noble descent, was the first to confront the Brahmans with the intention of converting them. He did this by presenting himself as a Brahman. Arriving in the southern Indian town of Madurai after lengthy preparation, he no longer bore any resemblance to those monks who travelled the land in tattered habits, hearing the confessions of the poor and the enslaved, and ringing their bells in fishing villages. Like the high-caste Hindus he wore a long robe of yellow linen, a turban on his head and wooden sandals on his feet.[20]

He continued to present himself as a consummate Brahman until the natives began to accept him, becoming prepared to listen to his delicately presented Christian teachings and, in the end, even to let him baptize them. In order to deal with the problem of exclusivity, he also made sure that the Yogi class were approached, the 'penitents' who were permitted to come into contact with every caste without becoming defiled:

> He suggested to his brethren that henceforth two missionary groups should be created, the one presenting themselves as Brahmans and the other as Yogis.[21]

This tactic proved more effective than any form of aggressive proselytizing: 'When Nobili departed, there were in the region over forty thousand converted indigenous people, among whom were many Brahmans', wrote Fülöp-Miller.[22]

To this day the Order renounces 'the wearing of monkish garb, dwelling in monasteries and the choral singing of divine office, in order to enable greater flexibility and unimpeded activities in all realms of ministry', we read in 'Ökumenisches Heiligenlexikon.de' (Ecumenical Holy Lexicon).

In short: The Jesuits transformed a missionary of the old school into an agent who:

— conformed and wore disguise,
— infiltrated and subverted,
— deceived and hoodwinked,
— gathered information (a spy),
— exerted influence.

The Jesuits eventually conquered the whole of Asia by this system. And not only Asia. All over the world they penetrated whole societies with their 'Jesuit style' and also rendered themselves indispensable at many royal courts. They assisted Asian rulers and likewise European rulers. And since every religious order also needs new recruits, they also founded schools and universities, doing a great deal of good on the one hand, but also increasing their power and influence on the other.

# Life's a game

The Jesuits regard the whole of life as a game in which they want to excel. Even today on their German website www.jesuiten.de they show a painting by the Catholic priest and painter Sieger Köder. It depicts three different clocks, which remind us of three different ages:

'The sundial of olden days, the sand clock or hour-glass of the Middle Ages, and the grandfather clock of nowadays. We are shown how time passes and how we ought to know "when the hour has struck",' the website explains. 'The foreground reminds us of a well-known song: "Life's a game; so when we play it, we shall reach the greatest aim".' This foreground depicts a game of cards, but interestingly instead of the usual jacks, queens and kings we have Martin Luther, Ignatius of Loyola, John XXIII, Francis of Assisi and various mighty and rich emperors. But the most interesting card of all is completely blank: 'The blank card is my card', says the Jesuit website: 'I may and I must join the game. The only question is: Which game do I play? The clocks tell us that the time has come!'

It was on a blank card of this kind that Joseph Hieronim Retinger once wrote his name. But despite all the information contained in Pomian's biography we still do not know what the founder of the Bilderbergers was at the start. And from Estulin we only learn in a subordinate clause that Winston Churchill was friends with 'Rettinger [sic], a Jesuit priest and 33 degree freemason'.

'A Jesuit priest and 33 degree freemason' – now this is beginning to sound interesting! And yet the real background of that inconspicuous Mr Retinger is mentioned only once in the whole of Pomian's book. And Estulin, too, concentrates more on Retinger's secret service activities, presenting, to be sure, many interesting and exciting facts. But without the Jesuit and Masonry aspects every-

thing still somehow lacks any firm foundation. Nevertheless, Estulin and von Rétyi both penetrate a good deal further than did Gary
Allen, once regarded as the pope of all conspiracy theorists who, in
his book *None Dare Call It Conspiracy*, published in 1972, first drew
a full picture of the global networks. For him, 'the man who created
the Bilderbergers is His Royal Highness Prince Bernhard of the
Netherlands'. Actually, nothing could be more incomplete. Not
once is Retinger's name mentioned in Allen's book.

When you think about it, surely a Jesuit initially remains entirely
a Jesuit and only subsequently becomes 'something secular'. Yes
indeed. The Jesuits were one of the first great and well-organized
secret societies, and they still are. But they do play a role in secular
secret services, and this will continue to be the case. That's what
makes sense.

### In the morass of 'conspiracy theories'

The Society of Jesus would, of itself, surely object to being included
among 'conspiracy theories'. The Order has been in existence for
five hundred years (or, more exactly: since 1534, or rather 1540
when it was confirmed as the Society of Jesus by a Papal Bull). This
is rather more ancient than those who seek to play down these
things, branding historical facts as 'conspiracy theories' – because
they either cannot or do not want to understand them. The Jesuits
are, for example, considerably more ancient than the notorious
Illuminati founded in 1776 by Adam Weishaupt. Actually it is more
accurate to see the Illuminati as an offshoot of the Jesuits. Their
'master' was a Jesuit, just as, much later on, Joseph Hieronim
Retinger was the founder of the Bilderbergers. Weishaupt was a
pupil at the Jesuit school of Ingolstadt in Germany. Although he is
said to have quarrelled with the Jesuits, this may be nothing but a
myth, so in reality the Illuminati might still be a 'planned daughter
movement' of the Jesuits. Whatever the case may be, they did

originate from the Jesuits, whether planned or not. It is hardly possible to deny that the secret society of the Illuminati had its source in Weishaupt's 'Jesuit know-how'. If they were not a Jesuit foundation, then Weishaupt founded 'his own Jesuits'.

So here we are, stuck in the midst of a 'morass of conspiracy theories'. How can this have happened, seeing that we've been following an entirely direct route? Evidently it's not a matter of 'conspiracy' at all, but rather one of historical facts which someone is trying to persuade us to ignore by means of the 'argument' that these facts are 'conspiracy theories'. There has been nothing irrational, mystical or ideological about our thinking. So someone who attempts to brand certain historical facts as 'conspiracy' must be endeavouring to discredit them. And who might have a greater interest in doing this than the conspirators themselves? 'The first job of any conspiracy, whether it be in politics, crime or within a business setting, is to convince everyone else that no conspiracy exists', wrote Gary Allen.[23]

The allegation of a 'conspiracy theory' is, then, the first indication that a conspiracy does exist.

But let us return to the Jesuits, that five-hundred-year-old powerful Catholic Order which promoted globalization initially and very successfully in the form of a Christian mission. It contrasted the brutal oppression of earlier times with gentle spiritual infiltration – and won. And from the Jesuits there emerged other sinister societies, such as Weishaupt and his Illuminati. This, in turn, is also no secret, but rather something that can happen with any organization.

# The keyboard of cultures

Evidently no language and no culture exists to which the Jesuit missionaries were unable to adapt completely. Neither borders between states nor borders between cultures existed for them. They were masters at playing upon the keyboard of cultures, and by their daily activities they negated both: the culture and its nation, which did not at all please the latter.

From the start the Jesuits had a problem with the nations, and the nations with them. Even on the Jesuits' website we read: 'The international character of the Order stood in opposition to the self-awareness which nation states had developed...' This demonstrates a degree of tension between the Jesuits and the nation states. The nation states feel threatened by the Order. So over the course of its history this Order, to which the Bilderbergers hark back, has again and again been outlawed.

Despite all their outer show of amiability, the reputation of the Jesuits deteriorated year by year. Critics began to discover in them something just as bad, or even worse, than the brutality of earlier missionary schools. This was their propensity for unscrupulous intrigue combined with moral duplicity and a flexible ethic.

In 1773 none other than Pope Clement XIV abolished the Order for the first time. In the nineteenth century the Church permitted its reinstatement, but it was then banned in numerous countries such as Norway, Switzerland and Germany (by Reich Chancellor Otto von Bismarck). In Switzerland it was proscribed until 1973. But on the other hand, it was not forbidden in the Third Reich, although 'as early as April 1935 the Gestapo in Munich ordered a critical watch to be kept on the sermons and lectures of the Jesuits', as the Society's website tells us. The headcount of victims in German provinces with a high Jesuitical population was 'high' during the

Third Reich. 'Three Jesuits were executed, one died during the night before his execution, three died in the camps, two were victims of euthanasia, 13 lost their lives as a result of the war, 79 never returned home after the war.'

Actually, in comparison with other persecuted groups, the Jesuits thus got off rather lightly. Moreover, the website doesn't claim that those Jesuits were persecuted on account of their membership of the Order. There was no systematic persecution of Jesuits during the Third Reich. Even open opposition to National Socialism was not what threatened the life of one particular Jesuit, as is demonstrated by the famous pastor Rupert Mayer. Although people like to regard him as 'the' church martyr in the Third Reich, the reality looks very different.

After speaking out early on about 'the dangers of National Socialism as it developed' and 'warning people about that movement', Mayer was arrested for the first time by the Nazis in January 1937 and sentenced to six months in prison, we read in Ökumenisches Heiligenlexikon.de. 'Because of "conspiratorial contacts" he was re-arrested in November 1939, received a number of sentences and was then subjected to seven months' solitary confinement at the Sachsenhausen concentration camp.' From 1940 until the end of the war he then had to remain in the comfortable monastery of Ettal under special supervision by the Gestapo. That Mayer escaped relatively lightly was partly down to the 1933 'Reich Concordat' between the Holy See and Germany guaranteeing the continued independence of the Catholic Church during the Third Reich, which not only granted the Church the right to raise taxes but also gave it considerable guarantees. For example the clergy enjoyed the same protection as the civil servants of the Third Reich (Article 5).

In Mayer's case, people are prone to overlook the fact that rather than being exposed to special persecution he actually enjoyed special protection. In reality, Jesuits were handled with kid gloves: 'In 1941 Hitler promulgated the secret order exempting all Jesuits from active military service and granting them indefinite leave.'

(jesuiten.org: history post-1773). This was at a time when military service not unusually signified certain death.

## Monita secreta — the secret instructions of the Jesuits

Why am I recounting all this?

Well, as I've already said, the Jesuits were the first modern globalists. The desire to conquer by means of their 'dictatorship through clemency' was from the start inimical to the national state. Let's remember their motto: 'Life's a game; so when we play it, we shall reach the greatest aim.'

Might this also be the Bilderbergers' motto? Are the Bilderbergers perhaps a belated confirmation of all the judgements and prejudices against the Jesuits? Do the Bilderbergers perhaps provide vindication for every prohibition ever promulgated against the Jesuits?

The most important source of the negative image of the Jesuits is the *Monita secreta* (*Secret Instructions*), their most famous document in which their fifth Superior-General, Claudio Acquaviva, supposedly instructed his subordinates to use literally every means to increase the power and prosperity of the Order. Can we perhaps rediscover the Bilderbergers in this document which an online-lexicon says: '. . . recommends, for example, the gaining of influence over the great and the powerful of this world'? The Jesuits were to 'fabricate intrigues and work through conspiracy, to exercise influence unlawfully over politics, to receive secret instructions from abroad, and to be unscrupulous in their choice of method and lax in their morals'.

Governments and monarchs have indeed always regarded the Jesuits as especially dangerous conspirators against the national state. So the suspicion that the Bilderbergers, founded by a Jesuit, may be aiming to form a world government, fits the picture rather well.

On the other hand, there is also a rumour that the *Secret*

# SECRET INSTRUCTIONS

## OF

# THE JESUITS,

FAITHFULLY TRANSLATED FROM THE LATIN OF AN
OLD GENUINE LONDON COPY,

WITH

## AN HISTORICAL SKETCH,
&c. &c.

### BY W. C. BROWNLEE, D. D.
OF THE COLLEGIATE REFORMED DUTCH CHURCH.

NEW-YORK:
AMERICAN AND FOREIGN CHRISTIAN UNION,
156 Chambers-street, a few doors West of the
Hudson River Rail Road Depot.

1857.

*Title page of an edition of the Jesuits' Monita secreta dated 1924*

*Instructions* are a forgery. The fact that this assertion stems from circles close to the Jesuits does not simplify the matter, since it makes it appear as though they themselves are the source of the rumour. The only way to settle the matter is to examine those *Secret Instructions*. Can we, for example, detect in them the Jesuit policies described above, or are we indeed reminded of the behaviour of Retinger, the Bilderberger's founder, or of the secretive Bilderberg group itself? The authenticity of a document can be judged not only by its source and history but also by the validity of the way it presents a specific phenomenon or indeed reality as a whole.

## CHAPTER II.

*In what manner the Society must deport, that they may work themselves into, and after that preserve a familiarity with princes, noblemen, and persons of the greatest distinction.*

I. Princes, and persons of distinction every where, must by all means be so managed that we may have their ear, and that will easily secure their hearts: by which way of proceeding, all persons will become our creatures, and no one will dare to give the Society the least disquiet or opposition.

*Monita secreta: How to win the friendship of princes and persons of distinction*

Chapter II of the *Monita secreta* is concerned with: 'In what manner the Society must deport, that they may work themselves into, and after that preserve a familiarity with princes, noblemen, and persons of the greatest distinction.' Of princes, noblemen and persons of greatest distinction? This sounds just like a 'wanted placard' published by the Bilderbergers; they, too, offer a tryst not only to princes and prominent personages but also to all kinds of nobility right up to monarchies. Then follows a reasonably accurate description of how Bilderberger founder Retinger behaved: 'Princes, and persons of distinction everywhere, must by all means be so managed that we may have their ear, and that will easily secure their hearts: by which way of proceeding, all persons will become our creatures, and no one will dare to give the Society the least disquiet or opposition.' There is both a defensive and an offensive aspect to this formulation.

What then follows is a perfect description of Jesuit tactics as applied earlier by Franz Xavier toward the Brahmans: 'Above all, due care must be taken to curry favour with the minions and domestics of princes and noblemen; whom by small presents, and many offices of piety, we may so far bypass, as by means of them to get a faithful intelligence of the bent of their master's humours and inclinations.'

And in Chapter II, paragraph 15 we read: 'Finally, — Let all with such artfulness gain the ascendant over princes, noblemen, and the magistrates of every place, that they may be ready at our beck, even to sacrifice their nearest relations and most intimate friends, when we say it is for our interest and advantage.' The sum total of all these instructions is: infiltrate and penetrate — exactly what Franz Xavier did with the Brahmans.

## CHAPTER III.

*How the Society must behave themselves towards those who are at the helm of affairs; and others who, although they be not rich, are notwithstanding in a capacity of being otherwise serviceable.*

I. All that has been before mentioned, may, in a great measure, be applied to these ; and we must also be industrious to procure their favor against every one that opposes us.

*Monita secreta: How to conduct oneself in relation to powerful statesmen*

By developing relationships with servants and valets de chambre (especially those of noble women and princesses), by hearing confession and by influencing marriage and matchmaking between princely houses, and by obtaining dispensations with regard to impediments to marriage (for example in the case of blood relationships), the Jesuits should make themselves indispensable to the noble houses. Associations like the Bilderbergers might profitably refer to Chapter II, paragraph 11:

> It will be very proper to give invitations to such to attend our sermons and fellowships, to hear our orations and declamations, as also to compliment them with verses and theses; to address them in a genteel and complaisant manner, and at proper opportunities to give them handsome entertainments.

As already mentioned, it is intended that the Bilderbergers should contribute officially to the attainment of an understanding between the USA and Europe and help to prevent conflicts. This is fittingly expressed in Chapter II, paragraph 12 and Chapter XVII of the *Monita secreta*:

> Let proper methods be used to get knowledge of the animosities that arise among great men, that we may have a finger in reconciling their differences; for by this means we shall gradually become acquainted with their friends and secret affairs, and of the necessity to engage one of the parties in our interests... Let kings and princes be kept up in this principle, that the Catholic faith, as matters now stand, cannot subsist without civil power, which however must be managed with the greatest discretion. By this means our members will work themselves into the favour of persons in the highest posts of government, and consequently be admitted into their most secret councils.

In accordance with these instructions, the strategy of the Jesuits pointed, or indeed points, in two directions:

1. Gaining inside knowledge (input)
2. Manipulation (output)

Or, if we want to repeat the secret service jargon used earlier:

1. Espionage
2. Exercising influence

How does one sound out powerful men? Simple: Set up a discussion group of powerful men. For the second reason alone the establishment of the Bilderbergers could have been worthwhile for the Jesuits, since their Brother Retinger participated for six years in those same clandestine meetings which he himself had set in train. Whether and in what way the Jesuits still participate in those meetings will be investigated later.

The founding of the Bilderbergers as an 'instrument for rapprochement and reconciliation' after World War II gives us much food for thought. According to the *Monita secreta*, if there is no other way of attaining the aims of the Jesuit Order, then 'schemes must be cunningly varied, according to the different posture of the times; and princes, our intimates, whom we can influence to follow our councils, must be pushed on to embroil themselves in vigorous wars one with another, to the end, our Society (as promoters of the universal good of the world) may on all hands be solicited to contribute its assistance, and always employed in being mediators of public dissensions: by this means the chief benefices and preferments in the church will, of course, be given to us by way of compensation for our services.'(Chapter XVII, paragraph 8) Were the Bilderbergers perhaps intended to be such an 'instrument for reconciliation'?

A large part of the *Monita* is concerned with the third aim of the order, namely 'reaping the benefits', i.e. how the outwardly poor Society of Jesus might increase its wealth. The Jesuits had their eye especially on rich widows. How to surround rich widows with Jesuit father confessors and suitable servants is the subject of quite a number of instructions contained in the *Monita secreta*, so much so, indeed, that one might almost rename it 'Moneta' secreta. The widows were to be guided towards making donations and doing other good deeds for the Society; and one was of course especially instructed to utter the highest praise with reference to the state of widowhood itself. Nothing is worse than a new master of the house. So widows were to occupy their time with spiritual exercises and thus hold off any suitors. Another ploy was to borrow money from rich men against certificates of indebtedness. Repayment was then to be put off for a long time until, for example, the creditor fell seriously ill. He was to be shown great consideration and attention until he could be ensnared into handing back the credit note (without the debt having been repaid, it goes without saying). This was preferable to waiting for testamentary donations, since one did not thereby attract the hatred of the heirs.

We can of course easily draw our own conclusions concerning the 'morality' of these instructions. They belong to the high art of manipulation, or rather: the highest art of manipulation in its most malicious and spiteful form: 'Lastly, let the women who complain of the vices or ill-humour of their husbands, be instructed secretly to withdraw a sum of money, that by making an offering thereof to God, they may expiate the crimes of their sinful help-mates, and secure a pardon for them'. (Chapter IX, paragraph 16)

If the 'Moneta' or rather the *Monita secreta* are genuine, we shall be obliged to conclude that the Society of Jesus is nothing other than a highly dangerous power-seeking and money-making machine functioning under the guise of sanctity. But of course it is not intended that we should see this, for the goods and possessions of the Society are to be most carefully kept out of sight and hidden away. The instructions are reminiscent of a money-making machine in religious disguise such as exist in many a sect. Included in this are the harsh disciplinary measures against members who put the wealth of the Society at risk. Religious piety here serves solely to squeeze money out of the faithful in exchange for indulgences and the promise of forgiveness. Although in this respect the Jesuits walk hand in hand with the Catholic Church as a whole, they appear to have developed it to a special degree of perfidiousness.

The modest or even poverty-stricken demeanour of the members of the Order thus serves solely as a cover for their true avarice and the Order's financial power.

## CHAPTER XVI.

### *In what manner we must outwardly feign a contempt of riches.*

**I. Lest the seculars should represent us as too much hankering after riches, it will be proper now and then to refuse such small and trifling alms as are offered for performance of pious offices; though of such as are thoroughly attached to our interest, we must readily accept whatever they give us, lest we bring upon ourselves the imputation of covetousness for our swallowing nothing but presents of value.**

*Monita secreta: Poverty and modesty as a disguise for an Order obsessed with power?*

So Chapter XVI of the *Monita* talks of 'outwardly feigning a contempt for riches': 'Lest the seculars should represent us as too much hankering after riches, it will be proper now and then to refuse such small and trifling alms ...' but not, of course, the more substantial offerings.

'2. Let burial in our churches be denied to persons of a base character, although, in their life-times, they have been ever so much our friends, lest the world should surmise that we hunt after riches by the number of the deceased ...' Especially those who are more devoted, such as widows or other wealthy persons, must be sternly treated 'lest people should imagine their greater indulgence proceeds from hopes of secular advantages'.

The *Monita secreta* as described here are nothing other than a set of Machiavellian instructions for the attainment of absolute power. It would not be an exaggeration to regard an order of this kind as a highly threatening conspiracy. Might this be the reason for the numerous bans levied against the Jesuits over the course of time?

'Between 1555 and 1931 the Society of Jesus was expelled from at least 83 countries, city states and cities, for engaging in political intrigue and subversion plots against the welfare of the State, according to the records of a Jesuit priest of repute', writes the Canadian historian J.E.C. Shepherd. 'Practically every instance of expulsion was for political intrigue, political infiltration, political subversion, and inciting to political insurrection.' (Shepherd, J.E.C. *The Babington Plot: Jesuit Intrigue in Elizabethan England*, Toronto, Canada, Wittenburg Publications.)

Really? Many sources tell us that the *Monita secreta* are a forgery. Others describe them as a 'satirical document'. If these assertions are true, they are a pretty good forgery or satire. The tactics and procedures they describe are convincing, reproducible and consistent. And in addition they are entirely compatible with Joseph Hieronim Retinger, founder of the Bilderbergers:

— modest to poverty-stricken behaviour,
— contacts and associations with the highest to topmost circles,
— organization of the 'sermons and fellowships', 'social meetings', 'talks', 'negotiations', 'orations and declamations' and 'handsome entertainments' as mentioned in the *Monita secreta*.

In accordance with the *Monita secreta* these activities were to be set in train without any compulsion, for compulsion leads to:

— definition of oneself and others,
— dissociation,
— the establishment of barriers.

Barriers are a person's demarcation lines and thus not at all desirable from the point of view of ideologies such as imperialism or organizations like the Society of Jesus which set their sights on expansion. Since expansion has to take place to the detriment of other individuals or other states, it is desirable for their barriers to disappear. This is the purpose, for example, of systems of states such as the European Union which in this way dissolves dozens of states at a stroke while preparing for their take-over by a global system.

Confrontations are detrimental to this process because they lead to the setting-up instead of the removal of barriers. According to the *Monita secreta*, it is important to strive for the allure of a special event and for the attainment of consensus through flattery. Whereas the concept of pressure and coercion aims to create first pressure and then consensus (through submission), the concept of the *Monita* generates first consensus and then manipulation. It is far easier to manipulate someone who regards you as a friend rather than an enemy. Pressure and coercion, instead of consensus, can very quickly lead to the opposite result and therefore failure, because the other person first recognizes his own interests and is then able to set his own limits. True manipulation, which is not even easily recognizable by the participant, remains entirely unnoticed by third parties. And such manipulation is, in effect, also very much more durable and long-lasting than domination by force or constraint. In the latter case, the situation may continue to smoulder in the victim, so that he will be likely to seize the first opportunity to break free.

# The path to world domination

Dispute about the Jesuits has been raging for centuries. 'There are thousands of works about the Society of Jesus... But among all those writings there are only a few by authors who have endeavoured to give an objective account of their subject. The majority set out either to mock and accuse, or to defend and praise.'[24]

The author of this quote, René Fülöp-Miller, decided not to take sides in his description. The result is a fascinating history of the Jesuit Order in which the approach, the intention and the methods of the Jesuits are clearly revealed. Chapter headings such as 'Behind a Thousand Masks', 'Merchant with Merchant', 'Soldier with Soldier', 'Dictatorship of Clemency', 'Comedy of Disguises' and 'The Path to World Domination' speak a plain language. Fülöp-Miller describes the Jesuit career path as leading from preacher to father confessor to confidential friend of the mighty:

> As they came to acquire ever greater numbers of penitents they began to realize that not only power over the souls of the masses was important but also above all domination over those very few individuals in influential positions on whom the destiny of nations depended. It was only when they had gradually gained mastery over the consciences of kings and princes that the Jesuits' actual political role could commence. The path to world domination, which had begun with friendly acts of human kindness and developed into organized works of social benefaction, moved on to new goals as the activities of the Order turned increasingly to the spiritual guidance of those princes. For it was in such princes that the Jesuit Order now saw the personification of a nation as a whole.[25]

Quite a neat trick. By treating the interests of the ruler as the equivalent of the interests of the people, one leads oneself and others to suppose that in influencing the rulers one is serving the welfare of the whole. But apart from this, Fülöp-Miller is anyway presupposing that world domination is what the Jesuits are actually aiming for. Even Ignatius of Loyola, the founder of the Order, he says, had 'very early on clearly recognized the mission in world history of the Society he had created':

> When the Jesuits of Cologne had spent rather too much time ministering to the rural population, Ignatius expressly repri-manded them, writing that such activities were only necessary at the beginning. There was nothing worse than running after such small successes while losing sight of greater tasks; Jesuits were not to strive only for the conversion of the rural masses but should set their sights much higher. And those higher sights chiefly involved winning over and permanently influ-encing both the secular and the spiritual rulers ...[26]

This says it all about the meaning and purpose of those secret Bilderberg Conferences. Not that every participant should pour his heart out to a Jesuit — the mechanics of power have meanwhile developed considerably and become much more diversified. But it was surely no coincidence that these conferences were set in train by a Jesuit monk — and the Bilderberg Conferences were not the only meetings. It appears that the Jesuits have a fitting organization for every type and level. They have founded, or participated in founding, quite other gatherings than those of the Bilderbergers. So our Jesuit Joseph Hieronim Retinger was indeed a true pike in a fishpond. He knew not only Prince Bernhard of Holland but also numerous sinister personages in the USA, all those well-known imperialists and globalists of his day, from Nelson and David Rockefeller and CIA boss Allen Dulles (whose nephew Avery was a Catholic cardinal and Jesuit), Walter Bedell Smith (Eisenhower's chief of staff and one of the first directors of the CIA), Thomas

Braden (a CIA agent), and right on to the legendary CIA boss William 'Wild Bill' Donovan, who by the way had also been educated at an equally strict Catholic school.

Since Retinger died in 1960, one might now tend to see the Jesuit influence on the Bilderbergers as having reached its conclusion. But this is not the case. The Jesuits run a huge network of educational establishments for the elite, mostly in the USA. 'Jesuit schools are one of the most effective apostolic activities of the Society of Jesus in the United States', the Jesuits' US website states. 'Jesuits and their (lay) colleagues educate over 46,000 boys and girls every year in 71 secondary or pre-secondary schools.' And this is not all. Thirty universities and colleges are members of the American Association of Jesuit Colleges and Universities. There are no fewer than 3,730 Jesuit educational establishments worldwide, with 2.5 million pupils and students (Source: jesuit.org). Thus the Jesuits' influence, especially on elite and ambitious sectors of society, is globally huge. It goes without saying that many of these pupils and students eventually arrive at the highest echelons – and thus also among the Bilderbergers.

Let's have a look at American conference participants since 1991. For example Bilderberger William McDonough, from 1993 to 2003 CEO of the Federal Reserve Bank of New York. After that he served as a 'special adviser' to the director of the finance conglomerate Merrill Lynch. McDonough attended the notorious Jesuit Georgetown University (which educated many bankers, military and secret service personnel) and also the College of the Holy Cross – another Jesuit institution. His predecessor at the New York Federal Reserve, E. Gerald Corrigan, attended two Jesuit universities, Fairfield and Fordham. Another student at Georgetown was Bill Clinton, subsequently US President and also a Bilderberger. At Georgetown he attended the Edmund Walsh School of Foreign Service, named after the Jesuit priest Edmund A. Walsh. It was at this School that Henry Kissinger was a professor from the late 1970s. EU Commissioner (from 1985) Peter D. Sutherland, member of the Steering Committee of the Bilderbergers and of the Trilateral Commission, was educated at the Jesuit Gonzaga College in Dublin. Following a typical Jesuit career, he became General Director of GATT, the free trade organization which sought to do away with national borders and from which the World Trade Organization later emerged. The former Belgian Prime Minister and Bilderberger attended the Sint-Jozefscollege at Aalst, Belgium. US Senator (Connecticut) and Bilderberger Christopher J. Dodd attended the Jesuit Georgetown Preparatory School and served as an ambassador under President Clinton. Dodd's eldest brother was a professor at Georgetown University. Thomas S. Foley, former US Ambassador (to Japan), ex-Speaker of the House of Representatives and Bilderberg attendee, went to the Jesuits' Gonzaga Preparatory School at Spokane. Former Prime Minster of the Netherlands and Bilderberger Ruud Lubbers attended the Jesuit Canisius College at Nimwegen, Holland. Bilderberger and temporary EU Commissioner Mario Monti attended the Jesuit L'Istituto Leone XIII in Milan. The well-known Bilderberger, publicist and founder of the *National Review*, William F. Buckley attended Beaumont College, a Jesuit school in England.

The following are members of the teaching staff at the Jesuit Georgetown University who are regular guests at Bilderberg conferences:

- Sally A. Shelton, Senior Fellow, Georgetown, widow of CIA Director William Colby (murdered 1996),
- Daniel K. Tarullo, Professor at Georgetown University,
- Casimir A. Yost, Professor at Georgetown University,
- Donald F. McHenry, Professor at Georgetown University,
- Peter F. Krogh, ex-Dean and Distinguished Professor at Georgetown University.

As has been said, these are only the American Bilderberg participants of the last twenty years. The Jesuits are likely to have provided similarly large contingents among the participants from other countries.

# Uniting the states of America

As we have already mentioned, the Jesuits have always added their influence at the very top with their monks and dignitaries being important actors in the great global game (which of course also on occasion caused the Order considerable bother as an important *global player* itself from the start). In order to gain a better understanding of the role of the Jesuits among the Bilderbergers we need to look more closely at a number of famous historical occurrences. For example, how did the American War of Independence come about? And why did the United States of America come into being anyway? One very simple reason was that the North American (Catholic) Jesuits centred in Maryland wanted to separate from the Anglican 'Motherland', Great Britain. For the 'soldiers of the Pope' the aim was simply to rescue the wonderful and immeasurably wealthy 'New World' from the English (Anglican) Church (headed by the British crown). British domination was threatening to extend its monopoly to North America. This was the *casus belli* for the Pope and his Jesuit warriors. And so the war began in 1775. The War of Independence was fought at least partially for religious reasons, which were of course also secular reasons, since power and money were what was at stake. But this is never mentioned. The only reason given was the intention of the British to impose taxation on the colonies. And the talk in public and in history is always only of men like John Adams (the second US President) who, together with his cousin Samuel, led the independence movement and finally founded the United States. Nevertheless, the Jesuits, who had taken over whole colonies such as Maryland, merrily joined in the fray.

Let us consider the Jesuit priest John Carroll. At the beginning of the Second Continental Congress (a kind of preliminary parliament consisting of delegates from the thirteen colonies) he endeavoured, together with his cousin Charles Carroll and a certain Benjamin Franklin, to persuade the French population of Canada to participate in the revolution against England. This mission failed, but Carroll's fellow travellers on the journey to Canada still became famous as the Founding Fathers of the United States. Franklin was a member of the Committee of Five which elaborated the 1776 Declaration of Independence, and John Carroll's cousin Charles was one of the signatories. Thus the Jesuits and also the Catholics in general had reached their goal, for the American Declaration of Independence also included a guarantee of religious freedom. John Carroll's elder brother Daniel, also a Founding Father, was one of the signatories. Thus Carroll and his family played a leading role in the separation of the British colonies in North America from Great Britain and also in the founding of the United States. The freedom and the unfolding personal liberty enshrined in the US Constitution served also to guarantee the freedom and free unfolding of the Jesuits and the Catholic Church. Thus Carroll also saved North America for the Pope and for his Order, the Jesuits. In 1789 Carroll's home, Baltimore, was declared the first diocese in the USA, and in the same year the Jesuit John Carroll was established as the first Catholic bishop of the United States. At around the same time Carroll founded Georgetown University. The first student, William Gaston, later became a member of Congress. Georgetown University and countless other Jesuit educational establishments came to play a major role in the education of American elites (see above). In no other country are there as many Christian zealots and fundamentalists as in the USA today. And an organized faith propaganda machine, in which self-selected (though not always Catholic) 'TV preachers' play a leading role, has meanwhile contributed to a regular 'religious dumbing down' of the United States.

# A Jesuit kingdom

The Jesuits have not only participated in forming states and in bringing about the downfall of states. They also created a state of their own, the 'socialist state of native Americans' in the region of present-day Argentina, Brazil and Paraguay. Their aim in doing this sort of thing was always the same, bringing smaller segments together to form larger unions. In the case of the United States, although the colonies split off from the motherland, it took only a century for the United States to cover the whole North American continent.

Bilderberg founder Retinger was also a fan of 'uniting states', not only in North America but also in Europe. It was not by accident that he studied ethnic psychology in Munich. First Joseph Hieronim Retinger (JHR) played a part in World War I, not as a soldier but as a puppet-master, remembers Jan Chciuk-Celt, a son of one of Retinger's friends. Even at that time the man had a wondrous measure of access to the highest circles, right up to the Kaiser:

> During the Great War JHR endeavoured to make use of his contacts in order to persuade Austria to leave the alliance together with Germany and make peace separately. This failed because the two Kaisers did not agree, and the result of his interference was that he seriously offended certain important personages. He was declared *persona non grata* in Austria, Great Britain no longer welcomed him, and the Germans wanted him dead, so he finally had to flee France without a penny and go to Spain. (Chciuk-Celt, Jan: *Jozef Hieronim Retinger 1888–1960*, updated 24 June 2009.)

He finally turned up in Mexico where he spent the greater part of the 1920s. And what did he do there? Well, he made the acquaintance of all the key figures in the country, trade union leaders, politicians and others. And, lo and behold! 'his good friend Calles became President of Mexico'. (Chciuk, ibid.)

For Retinger, however, this was no more than a way of passing the time. World War I was hardly over when he reappeared in Europe in order to continue with his machinations as a puppet-master. His first attempt at uniting the European states did, however, prove to be somewhat inept. As usual it was easy for him to arrange for an audience with the French President, Georges Clemenceau; but he failed to gain acceptance of his plan for a first 'European Union'. He suggested to Clemenceau that Austria, Hungary and Poland could be combined in a monarchy – under the leadership of the Jesuits! Perhaps this plan to increase the power and influence of the Jesuits was rather too obvious! Anyway, Clemenceau most certainly did not approve of the cat which had thus been let out of the bag, and Retinger was branded an agent of the Vatican.

# Uniting the states of Europe

Retinger did not want to make the same mistake twice. He spent World War II as a British agent in the battle for his homeland, Poland. Once the Third Reich had collapsed he realized that the time had come for him to resume his efforts for unification, but this time he was far more cautious and prudent. Rather than plant a fully-grown tree in the landscape, he made do with a seedling. In 1946, together with the Belgian Prime Minister, Paul van Zeeland, he founded the European League for Economic Cooperation (ELEC) and thus laid the foundation for a 'European movement'. Secretary General: the Jesuit Joseph Hieronim Retinger.

With his leading position in ELEC, JHR became one of the fathers, if not 'the' father, of the European Union and practically its first Secretary General.

Now, much has already been written about the two world wars. There is, however, one important aspect which led to sweeping global developments but which is not often mentioned. Both world wars were primarily seen by interested circles not as a means of defeating Germany, but as a means of doing away with the nation state as such. The concept of the nation state came to be permanently compromised by the two world wars. Doubts arose as to whether nations were at all capable of living peacefully in nation states; or should those nations be combined to form larger units? Something that initially appears to be rather obvious and noble is in reality a bizarre idea. What it actually means is the very opposite: a larger unit, a greater population and more resources enable a dictator to bring about even greater calamities at the stroke of a pen. Yet in reality balance can only be achieved through variety and decentralization. A clearer example would be that of a ship. The more watertight compartments it has, the less likely it is to sink, whereas a ship without bulk-heads, i.e. partitions, can be sunk by a single leak. But people like Retinger were suggesting the very opposite of this when they endeavoured to persuade humanity that borders should be abol-ished, in order to unite the nations in ever larger units so as to prevent new catastrophes. In reality, larger systems of states will always lead to greater catastrophes.

Retinger's efforts, however, concurred with the interests of the USA, now rendered more powerful than previously by World War II. The USA looked favourably on a European Union that would do away with the existing jumble of states, currencies and markets. Dozens of European states with their own border customs, security and food regulations posed considerable logistical problems. On the one hand they complicated the marketing of American products and on the other they stood in the way of a smooth establishment of American supremacy.

So the USA, too, were tinkering with a European union. The American fathers of the EU were recruited chiefly from among the geostrategists and secret service personnel already well-known to Retinger. Thus the American Committee for a United Europe (ACUE), founded in 1948, was financed chiefly by the Rockefeller Foundation, in other words by the same people who later partici-pated in founding the Bilderbergers. All the founders and members of the ACUE were good friends of our bustling intriguer, Jesuit Joseph Hieronim Retinger. Among them were:

— the notorious OSS veteran and CIA founder William 'Wild Bill' Donovan (OSS = Office for Strategic Services, forerunner of the CIA),
— Donovan's equally notorious OSS underling and subsequent boss of the CIA, Allen Dulles, uncle of the later Jesuit cardinal Avery Dulles,
— Walter Bedell Smith, the first director of the CIA,

and, not to be forgotten:

— Robert Ignatius Gannon, Jesuit and President of the Jesuitical Fordham University.

This murky troupe initiated the European Conference on Federation which was organized by Retinger at The Hague from 8 to 10 May 1948 and in which about eight hundred delegates from many European countries participated — none of whom were merely 'minor' deputies. Among them were no fewer than 18 former prime ministers and 28 former foreign ministers. Winston Churchill made the opening speech. So the Jesuit and Bilderberg founder, who was unknown to anyone publicly, succeeded in convening a gathering of eight hundred prominent personages for the purpose of setting the course for the unification of Europe. One might also put it this way: the Jesuit called and they all came, right up to the royal houses.

For a long time the ACUE was an important financial backer of the European movement. On 26 July 1950 secret service member William Donovan signed a memorandum containing instructions for the founding of the European Parliament.

Here we have the true roots of Europe and also of our trusty Bilderbergers.

It goes without saying that the official history of the European Union sounds quite different. The father of Europe is not some Retinger or other but Robert Schuman, born in Luxembourg, twice Prime Minster of France, and also Foreign Minister and Finance Minister. On 9 May 1950 he published the so-called Schuman Plan for the collaboration of the German and French coal and steel industries. On 18 April 1951 this became the European Community for Coal and Steel (ECCS). Over several decades this was then expanded, first as the European Economic Community (EEC) and then the European Union as we know it today. Like Konrad Adenauer, Schuman is nowadays a venerable saint before whom no European politician will forget to perform a rhetorical curtsy.

In his youth, Schuman attended Luxembourg's oldest and most prestigious gymnasium, the Athénée de Luxembourg, founded 350 years earlier by a Jesuit. And it was not by accident that he later joined the Christian (i.e. Catholic) Democratic Party in France. In 1958 he became the first President of the European Parliament, which had meanwhile come into being. In the same year he was awarded an honorary doctorate by the University of Leuven, which calls itself the oldest Catholic university in the world. It would perhaps be something of an exaggeration to describe Schuman as a Jesuit or Catholic agent if – and this does indeed beggar belief – there had not been some talk of beatification.

In 1988 a 'Federation of St Benedict for Europe' had applied to the Bishop of Metz for the beatification of Robert Schuman. Why might it be necessary for the Catholic Church to express its thanks to the founding father of the EU by means of a beatification?

The problem, however, was that this man had simply not accomplished a sufficient number of miracles. One more or less well vouched-for miracle (for example a miraculous healing) is required before a person can be beatified. The beatification proceedings continued to bumble along until 2004, but since then they appear to have been quietly dropped.

Time chart: The road to the European Economic Community (EEC)

| 9.5.1950 | Publication of the Schuman Plan for the collaboration of German and French coal and steel production |
| 26.7.1950 | William Donovan's memorandum on the foundation of the European Parliament |
| 18.4.1951 | Foundation of the European Community for Steel and Coal (ECSC) |
| 29–31.5.1954 | First Bilderberg Conference |
| 25.3.1957 | Signing of the EEC and EURATOM treaties |
| 1958 | Schuman becomes the first President of the European Parliament |

The next steps on the road to a unified Europe were the treaties for the European Economic Community (EEC) and the European Atomic Energy Community (EURATOM). These were signed by Belgium, the Federal Republic of Germany, France, Italy, Luxembourg and the Netherlands, not just anywhere, but in Rome, the 'capital city of Christianity' or, better, of the Catholic Church. 'Rain all day is expected for Rome on 25 March 1957', we read on a page from the (German) Federal Agency for Civic Education regarding the day of signing: 'Shortly before 1800 hrs the participating delegations arrived on the Capitoline Hill. Passing the equestrian statue of Marc Aurel they proceeded to the Palazzo dei Conservatori. Representatives of six governments took their seats in the grand Hall of the Horatians and Curiatians in order to set Europe on a new road... Foreign Minister Paul-Henri Spaak and General Secretary of the Brussels Ministry for Commerce Baron Jean-Charles Snoy et d'Oppuers for Belgium, Foreign Minister Christian Pineau and his Secretary of State Maurice Faure for France, Federal Chancellor Konrad Adenauer and Secretary of State for the Foreign Ministry Walter Hallstein for the Federal Republic of Germany, Minister President Antonio Segni and Foreign Minister Gaetano Martino for Italy, Secretary of State and Foreign Minister Joseph Bech and his Ambassador in Brussels Lambertus Schaus for Luxembourg and Foreign Minister Joseph Luns and Director for Mining at the Ministry for Commerce Johannes Linthorst Homan for the Netherlands signed the documents.'

Archival images of the event show the representatives of the signatory states seated like well-behaved schoolboys at a long table in the Hall of the Horatians and Curiatians. They look sheepish and dispirited in the midst of that enormous hall with its monumental murals depicting Rome's early history (Rape of the Sabine Women, Discovery of the Twin Brothers Romulus and Remus, etc.). At the end of the white signatory table, photos of the day show a larger than life sinister figure by the wall, in black. It may well be four or five times the height of a man. It's too black in the photos to be recognizable, and often it's almost eliminated by the way the picture has been trimmed. It looks as if it's greeting the cowed assembly with its right arm. This is the monumental bronze statue of Pope Innocent X. And on the other side of the room stood a statue of Pope Urban VIII.

*The monumental statue of Pope Innocent X blesses the Treaties of Rome*

In other words: The founding fathers of Europe came together as though watched over and blessed by two Catholic popes. Subsequently the hall was furnished with blue chairs showing the European flag's circle of stars – another Catholic symbol.

*The signatory hall of the Treaties of Rome with the papal statue and the blue, star-crowned chairs*

'For some it may be a pretty legend whereas for others it's an irrefutable fact: In 1955, after walking past a Madonna with the crown of stars, the Press Chief of the Council of Europe, Paul Levy, is said to have suggested using the circle of twelve stars; this was accepted and then later also used for the EU', we read in kirchengucker.de, a website on ecclesiastical art. This does sound rather arbitrary. Why didn't Paul Levy make all kinds of other suggestions after walking past one thing or another? In reality the flag of the European Union was purposely decorated with a Catholic symbol: the Mother of God's crown of stars.

'In those days of the 1950s, having been unsuccessful in getting their way about the use of the Cross, the Catholics responsible at the time for European affairs and designing the European flag settled instead for the circle of stars on a blue background, which were officially explained as signifying "Integrity and Unity"', wrote Professor Jürgen Newig. 'Evidently in order not to offend non-Catholics, the history of how the design came to be chosen remains somewhat shrouded. In *Die Welt* of 26 February 1998, Thomas Pinzka partially lifted this veil. According to him, Paul Levy, a Bel-

*Statue of the Madonna with the crown of stars; the European flag*

gian Jew who had converted to the Catholic faith and who at the time was head of the Culture Department of the European Council of Ministers, gave an interpretation of the flag's design after seeing a Madonna figure crowned with twelve golden stars. The draft by artist Arsène Heitz was approved by the Ministerial Committee of the Council of Europe on 8 December 1955, the day of the Festival of the Immaculate Conception of Mary, and published on the following day.'

The Council of Europe sanctions a symbol of devotion to the Madonna as the European flag? On the very day of the Immaculate Conception? A bizarre notion and yet it is true. And thereafter the flag of Europe was once more brought into proximity with the Madonna, as the motif of the eastern window of Strasbourg Minster which the states of Europe have donated to the Cathedral. This completes the circle. Is the European Union an ecclesiastical organization rather than a secular one? Or is it a secular organization belonging to the Church?

The Treaties of Rome, those milestones on the way to a European super-state, came into being under the auspices of none other than Jesuit Retinger's Bilderbergers. Or at least that's the cat which George McGhee, one of the central members of the early Bilderberg years and US Ambassador to Turkey and also to Germany, is said to have let out of the bag. With reference to the Bilderberg Conferences he reportedly claimed: 'I reckon you could say that the Treaties of Rome which ushered in the Common Market were born during those conferences.' Seen chronologically, the Treaties of Rome were signed only three years after the first Bilderberg Conference at Oosterbeek in Holland. (Many years later, in 1989, McGhee donated his Turkish villa in Alanya to the Jesuit Georgetown University.)

So the repeated claim of the Bilderberg Conferences being solely about 'an exchange of opinions', and not practical politics, is nothing more than a smokescreen. This is confirmed by a further example, that of the famous 'Four-Power Agreement' in Berlin in

1971. Here the former World War II allies, France, Great Britain, the USA and the Soviet Union, agreed the status of West Berlin as consisting of the western half of the former German capital city encircled by the German Democratic Republic (GDR). This Agreement also contained a guarantee of existence and regulations concerning traffic from and to West Berlin. When this Agreement was signed on 3 September 1971 in the premises of the Prussian Supreme Court at the Kleist-Park in Berlin-Schöneberg, it is unlikely that anyone realized that the Allies were merely confirming something which had been negotiated elsewhere, namely during the Bilderberg Conferences.

In 1993, the journalists Grazyna Fosar and Franz Bludorf participated at Potsdam in a discussion evening with the 'Society for the Founding of a Peace University in Berlin'. 'Three rather special political pensioners had a meeting: former American Secretary of State Henry Kissinger, former Soviet Ambassador to the GDR Valentin Falin, and Egon Bahr, personal adviser and chief negotiator to Willy Brandt, Federal German Chancellor in the 1960s and 1970s', said Fosar and Bludorf. 'They were reminiscing about the great days of German "Ostpolitik" and about the negotiations which had led to the agreement regarding the status of Berlin.'

It was one of those evenings when it was possible to make the most outrageous revelations without anyone noticing because the audience were more or less asleep anyway. Fosar and Bludorf were among those who stayed awake and were thus astonished to hear Kissinger make 'a momentous statement the significance of which probably bypassed most of the listeners': 'The four ambassadors [of the victorious powers of World War II, Ed.] did not have much negotiating to do in respect of the Berlin Agreement. They only had to sign the text prepared by the Bilderbergers.' (Fosar, Grazyna; Bludorf, Franz: *Die Bilderberger – Hinter den Kulissen der Macht* in: *Matrix3000*, Vol.25, Jan./Feb. 2005).

That was one of those fragments which from time to time find their way out of the Bilderberg Conferences and into the public domain.

But the Bilderbergers had their fingers in other pies as well. At least to some extent the 'expensive euro' can also be blamed on them. In 2009 one of the leading Bilderbergers, the Belgian industrial tycoon Étienne Davignon, stated that the Bilderberg Conference would be just as capable of improving people's understanding of the raging financial crisis as it had been in the 1990s of creating the euro in the first place. (Rettman, Andrew *'Jury's out on the future of Europe, EU doyen says'*, euobserver.com. 16.3.2009.)

In conclusion, then, let us record that firstly the Bilderbergers and secondly the European Union and its predecessors were Jesuit and therefore Catholic enterprises.

# The confidential reports of the Bilderbergers

By looking behind the scenes we can confirm the role played by the Bilderbergers in the founding of the European Union. Seven internal reports of Bilderberg Conferences leaked out between 1955 and 1980. From the very beginning, everything was intended to remain strictly confidential. 'As in the case of previous conferences, media access is not permitted. This document must be treated as strictly confidential; it is intended solely for the personal use of the recipient', begins the first of the seven reports, here referring to the conference at Garmisch-Partenkirchen from 23 to 25 September 1955. Not breathing a word was the order of the day. In opening the conference at Bürgenstock, Switzerland, from 28 to 29 May 1960, Prince Bernhard, the chairman, exhorted participants to 'remember the regulations governing Bilderberg Conferences and stressed the importance of avoiding leaks to the press'.

The leaked reports give a general outline of the agenda of each relevant conference and quote participants' contributions to the discussions without, however, mentioning a single name except that of the chairman.

Speakers appear in the reports solely as 'an American participant', 'a Canadian participant', or 'a European participant'. Rendered anonymous in this way, the reports manifest as being peculiarly unimportant and trifling. When the speaker is not named, the portent of the discussion remains unclear. One entirely forgets the degree of political and executive power that is holding forth: future and former heads of government, presidential advisers, foreign ministers and ministers of defence, CEOs and bankers, military leaders, presidents of international organizations such as the World Bank or the International Monetary Fund. At the end of the conference, all those heavyweights return home with the considerations of the Bilderbergers in mind, considerations which do not, of course, remain without influence on their decisions. 'Conference participants ought ... to be capable of making the insights reached accessible to public opinion in their own sphere of influence without revealing the source', stated one of the reports.

So after a conference every participant was to take the ideas of the Bilderbergers further without, however, letting on that those ideas stemmed from the Bilderberg club. In this way the Bilderbergers carried on, and continue to carry on, their involvement in geopolitics, economic and military politics, and also in influencing public opinion without anyone knowing whose influence is at work here.

The best way to describe this succession of conferences is, perhaps, to call it a strategic and executive 'think-tank' at the level of the European-American leadership; or even better: the 'brain of Euro-America'. The conferences resemble 'brainstorming sessions' among the trans-Atlantic elite, sessions with practical consequences. The participants in these brainstorming sessions have been and are, after all, those very decision-makers who are able subsequently to put the Bilderberg ideas and the Bilderberg consensus into action, from the General Secretary of NATO and on to ministers and future heads of government and finally to bosses of global giant conglomerates.

Yet what can a three-day meeting once a year be expected to achieve? The answer is that the work of the Bilderbergers is by no means restricted to those three days. Between the plenary conferences, for example, there are meetings of the steering committee of the Bilderbergers which is composed of the strategic hard-core of the group. In addition, discussion papers are distributed among the participants, so that they bring with them a whole bundle of preliminary material for the discussions. And finally, of course, different groups of Bilderbergers also meet one another during intervals between conferences at political or business meetings and projects, or else they are anyway members of the same executive bodies or committees of other organizations. In other words, this is not a matter of a single conference but of a whole process that has been in operation since 1954. When a Bilderberg Conference comes to an end the process is not interrupted in any way; instead, between meetings, it enters into a realization phase during which the participants act in accordance with the intentions of the Bilderbergers. In ideal cases, if one is a Bilderberger one acts in accordance with the Atlantic or, in the end, the globalist spirit.

# The 'Atlantic Community'

As can be gathered from the reports, the Bilderbergers have from the outset been pursuing two aims: to transform the European Union into a great association of states, and to unite the 'association' of Europe with the United States of America to form the so-called 'Atlantic Community' which, furthermore, would include the British Commonwealth, the OAS (Organization of American States), the United Nations and France with its former colonies. The logical consequence of this 'community' would be for it to encompass the whole world. The United Nations are the necessary tool for this. 'The creation and further development of the United Nations denote an irreversible process', said a speaker at the 1962 Bilderberg Conference at Saltsjöbaden. Unlike the League of Nations, the United Nations would have a universal task. 'Their aim to rule the world is a firm dimension.' It's quite understandable that one would not want to read a quote like this above one's own name.

*Imperial magnificence: the 1962 Bilderberg venue, the Grand Hotel at Saltsjöbaden, Sweden*

Two main themes dominated discussions about the 'Atlantic Community': How the USA and Europe differ and what they have in common. The differences were to be recognized and described and then dismantled while the similarities were to be emphasized and developed into shared strategies. Of course a first step towards coming closer together would have to involve the reduction of differences and tensions. So 'community' would, in the first instance, signify the recognition and reduction of any tensions between the USA and Europe. Reading a 1955 report, one might regard the Bilderbergers in the initial phase of the 1950s as an instrument for synchronization between the USA and Europe:

> The purpose of this series of conferences is to reach the highest possible denominator of mutual understanding between the countries of Western Europe and North America and so to work for the removal of causes of friction, to study those fields where action may be necessary to prevent friction from arising in the future, and to examine the general areas in which agreement may be sought... Nevertheless, it is a matter of the utmost urgency that the will and the means should exist for finding a common basis on which to build our future... It is believed also that in the wide and important field presented by the European-American Associations, much could be done towards creating the friendly atmosphere for the growth of the highest degree of co-operation.

As we have said, European unity was a matter of particular urgency for the Bilderbergers: 'The discussion on this subject revealed general support for the idea of European integration and unification among the participants from the six countries of the European Coal and Steel Community, and a recognition of the urgency of the problem.' It had been 'generally recognized that it was our common responsibility to arrive in the shortest possible time at the highest degree of integration, beginning with a common European market'. The final goal would be the 'unification of Europe'. They were also already beginning to think about the euro. 'A European speaker expressed concern about the need to achieve a common currency, and indicated that in his view this necessarily implied the creation of a central political authority.'

Only three years later the Treaties of Rome were signed.

# The North Atlantic Treaty Organization

The power of the Bilderbergers is not only political and of course also financial, but military as well. The regular attendance of the respective NATO General Secretary and of various defence ministers at the conferences bears this out. From its inception NATO was seen as a vehicle and an organization of European, and indeed American-European, unity. De facto NATO already puts Europe and the USA in command of a shared army. The Bilderbergers consider and decide upon all NATO's important issues, which are then dealt with by members relevant to NATO, above all its General Secretary. From the beginning, strategy towards the East was as much an item on the agenda as were internal psychological and propaganda issues: 'One of the functions of the Bilderberg group could consist in ensuring that members promote understanding within their own countries concerning NATO's mission with regard both to peace and to defence', states the 1955 conference report. One speaker had the impression that propaganda was not so important, but rather what NATO itself could do to inspire people and prepare them psychologically for the use of nuclear weapons, should this become necessary for their defence:

> It would be very useful if NATO officials could put pressure on their governments to prepare young people in the different countries for the task with which they would be confronted as members of NATO's armed forces. Some countries were tending to reduce the scale of armed forces they placed at the discretion of NATO; it is essential to observe these tendencies.

Bilderbergers have always reacted nervously to the possibility of NATO member states acting on their own authority. They ought always to consult the alliance before setting any 'unilateral' measures in train.

# The rest of the world

The architecture of nuclear deterrence has also frequently been a theme for Bilderberg Conferences. There were discussions about how this architecture might and should function, about the extent to which limited wars might be possible or could be expected, and about which factors they might threaten or support. As the brain of the 'Atlantic Community', the Bilderberg Conferences served not only the determination of one's own situation in the world but also the delineation of new strategies over against the rest of the world, i.e. towards the other large power blocks and institutions such as the Soviet Union, China, Africa and others. One problem that concerned the Bilderbergers was the transition of power in 1953 from the Soviet dictator Joseph Stalin to the 'more civilian' Party leader Nikita Khrushchev. For years the Bilderbergers ruminated about the changes and possible consequences this might bring about in the Soviet Union and in the world.

Other themes were disarmament, deterrence and rearmament as well as the 1960 U2-crisis, the 1962 Cuban Missile crisis, and the Iranian hostage crisis from 1979 to 1981. And in 1980, now over thirty years ago, the attention of the world and of the Bilderbergers was focussed on two regions which today are once again making us hold our breath: Iran and Afghanistan. In Iran the hostage-taking of US embassy personnel drew the attention of the Bilderbergers, whereas in Afghanistan it was that country's occupation by the USSR which, as it has since turned out, signalled the demise of the Communist empire. Regarding Africa, it was de-colonization, especially of the British colonies, on which the Bilderbergers spent a great deal of time. Colonialism was seen as an aberration of national interests; in future it was to be replaced by higher European or trans-Atlantic aims. Before globalization could come about, the world would first have to be rescued from the old national colonial structures. Other important themes for discussion were, of course, economic and financial questions such as customs tariffs, (free) trade, and currencies.

# Part 3

# A GLOBAL MAFIA?

'In order to avoid being accused of founding an unofficial political "mafia", we decided from the outset not to consider ourselves a policy-making body but to have as our principal aim the smoothing over of difficulties and tendencies among countries and the finding of a common approach in the various fields – political, cultural, economic, and social.'[27]

So the father of the Bilderbergers himself was the first to use the ominous word 'mafia' because he anticipated unavoidable associations and reproaches. However, to defend oneself can also amount to accusing oneself. Does the word 'mafia' perhaps actually provide a fitting portrayal of the Bilderberg club? What is a mafia? A mafia is an unofficial, informal club which pursues shared unofficial aims that reach beyond the immediate relationships of those involved. A mafia is:

– unofficial,
– informal (i.e. has no agreed forms),
– illegal,
– secret,
– discrete,
– unverifiable,
– not elected,
– characterized by mutual affiliations.

To be precise, the Bilderbergers don't actually meet all these criteria, e.g. illegality. But the characteristic of being unofficial and 'private', which they themselves commend, does very much suggest something threatening and it also provides the best fertile soil for sinister activities. It is the very nature of this unofficial and informal characteristic that is what is threatening. So wagging tongues might well reformulate Retinger's sentence quoted above as follows:

> In order not to be accused of founding an unofficial political 'mafia', we have founded an unofficial political mafia.

Whatever their differences, as with a mafia the actual stock in trade of the Bilderbergers is the same: they are discrete and they have contacts. In fact the scale of the Bilderberg network is breathtaking. It is impossible to describe the thousands of attendees or members and it would be a mammoth task to analyse the business relationships and links among them. So let's at least begin with an attempt at a quantitative assessment: Assuming that every Bilderberger holds or has held between 6 and 24 different positions (board of directors, executive director, top manager, top adviser, government post, professorship, etc.), i.e. on average 15, and that so far about 2,500 different persons have attended Bilderberg Conferences, we arrive at an estimated total of 37,500 positions which Bilderbergers hold or have held. The number of useful contacts open to such 'contact giants' would surely be far higher; if we work with a factor of ten we arrive at 375,000. But contacts represent only one aspect of the Bilderbergers. The other is the financial power they represent. The bankers, CEOs, ministers of finance and investors together control untold billions. Take Royal Dutch Shell alone, in which Bilderberg founder Prince Bernhard of the Netherlands and his daughter, Bilderberg member Queen Beatrix, held or hold shares; with half a billion dollars of annual turnover it is the largest company in the world, yet it is only one of hundreds in which Bilderbergers exercise their influence, either by being on boards of directors or by holding shares. This means that the Bilderberg network is likely to be qualitatively as well as quantitatively one of the most powerful networks ever. The Bilderbergers most certainly represent an exceedingly important power centre worldwide.

So who belongs to this 'global mafia'?

As already mentioned, the largest number of attendees at all Bilderberg Conferences are from the USA. One third are from the USA and the others from Europe. The US participants are central, arch-reactionary strategists such as Henry Kissinger, Richard Perle, David Rockefeller, Richard Holbrooke, Vernon E. Jordan, Colin Powell, Paul Wolfowitz, Alan Greenspan, George Soros, Donald Rumsfeld, Henry Paulson and many others. These are the circle whose members are responsible not only for the financial crisis but also for the USA's dirty wars from the Korean War in the 1950s, the Vietnam War in the 1960s and early 1970s, and right on to those following on from 11 September 2001. On 26 January 1998, the 'neo-conservatives' Paul Wolfowitz, Richard Perle and Donald Rumsfeld wrote to the then US President Bill Clinton suggesting that it was high time to initiate a more offensive policy towards the Near East so as to remove Saddam Hussein from his post – or would Clinton, perhaps, prefer to be removed from his? Well, they didn't actually say this in so many words, but they dropped the hint. As it hadn't been possible to remove him after the Lewinsky affair, they had to wait until 11 September 2001, which at last relieved them of the need to wait any longer. The USA then proceeded to march into Afghanistan as well as Iraq. It was US Secretary of State Colin Powell who, in 2003, sold the deception about Iraq's presumed weapons of mass destruction to the UN Security Council. Almost all these war-mongers are to be found among the Bilderbergers. Robert B. Zoellick, Vin Weber, William Kristol and Robert Kagan were further signatories to the just-mentioned threatening letter to President Clinton.

In other words, leading Bilderbergers are at the same time among the leading swindlers and war-mongers of our planet.

The list below shows the most frequent participants at Bilderberg Conferences in the nineteen years from 1991 to 2009. It is based on the official participant lists and is thus neither entirely accurate nor complete. It shows participants who attended at least 15 times, and it was convenient to include members of the same family as a group. Thus Henry R. and Marie-Josée Kravis became 'Family Kravis', David and Sharon Rockefeller became 'Family Rockefeller', and Jacob and Markus Wallenberg became 'Family Wallenberg':

| Name | 1991 to 2009 attendances at the Bilderbergers |
|---|---|
| Family Kravis | 25 |
| Family Rockefeller | 23 |
| Halberstadt, Victor | 20 |
| Davignon, Étienne | 19 |
| Queen Beatrix of the Netherlands | 17 |
| Wolfensohn, James D. | 16 |
| Family Wallenberg | 15 |

*(Estimate – no guarantee)*

# The grand old man

That's David Rockefeller. To many, the name of Rockefeller sounds just as fusty as that of Kissinger. Both are regarded as bugbears from the long gone days of early capitalism and imperialism, when people's conceptions of the world were still as clear as were the images of their foes. In the nineteenth and twentieth centuries the name of Rockefeller was akin, in the USA, to that of Croesus, the mythical last king of Lydia in the days of ancient Greece and Rome. For decades, if not centuries, the Rockefellers were the leading oil and banking dynasty of the United States and the very embodiment of the most savage capitalism and imperialism. In 2009, 94-year-old David Rockefeller was the successor of John D. Rockefeller, whose huge company Standard Oil behaved so badly, even by American norms, that it was broken up in 1911. This had not, however, done much to reduce the influence of the Rockefellers. Companies such as Mobil Oil, Exxon, Chevron, Amoco and Conoco are among Standard Oil's successors.

The Rockefellers – whose mining concern CF&I fought pitched battles with its employees in 1914 (Ludlow Massacre) during which, according to *Who's Who*, women and children were burnt to death – disguised their appalling reputation under an illusion of truth, beauty and goodness, just as did Kissinger. 'In order to mend his reputation in public, Rockefeller distributed generous donations in various fields', says *Who's Who*. 'Rockefeller established charitable institutions, set up social endowments and created the "Rockefeller Foundation" which exists to this day.' (*Who's Who*: John D. Rockefeller.) People always promulgate the propaganda of which they are most in need.

In short: The more saintly and peace-loving a person's pose, the greater the aggressiveness he seeks to hide. This is true not only of the Catholic Church but equally of many a Nobel Peace Prize winner and 'philanthropist'. So: Beware 'philanthropists'! They can be found by the ton among the Bilderbergers. But, that said, if one looks more closely at the concept of 'philanthropy' (the love of human beings) one anyway gains a sense of something being out of kilter. Who loves people *per se* unless he or she is a saint? Normally both love and hate express a relationship with a specific person. Someone who loves a whole 'species' is elevating himself above that species, for example a dog or cat lover, a stock breeder, or a butterfly collector.

The Rockefellers paint themselves up to be 'philanthropists', and they finance numerous foundations, which in the long run continue to pursue their imperialistic aims under the guise of the common good. 'I enjoy meeting people', says David Rockefeller, a descendant of that Capitalist Baron. He built up his family's Chase Manhattan Bank (which has meanwhile ceased to exist) to be, for a while, the largest bank in the world. (See *Süddeutsche Zeitung*, 3.4.2008) And from 1985[28] he led the American Council on Foreign Relations (CFR), the USA's foreign policy think-tank, a collective of America's richest and most powerful individuals.

# Excursus: The 'Council on Foreign Invasions'

The Council on Foreign Relations is a kind of revolving door, or circling conveyor belt, between banks, the oil industry, large concerns, governments and secret services. Practically all influential US politicians (and of course also Henry Kissinger) and most US presidents, including Barack Obama, are recruited from it. The CFR is the source from which mind-games such as the 'Clash of Civilizations' emerged, the idea that the East-West conflict will be succeeded by a religious conflict between occident and orient, i.e. between Christianity and Islam. This idea was urgently needed because the East-West conflict from which the USA had gained both distinction and profit had suddenly vanished. A certain Samuel Huntington first published the idea in 1993 in the Council's journal *Foreign Affairs* and then as a book.[29] This was at a time when no-one could have imagined or wanted a war of cultures, apart from the US-*imperium* which was looking for a new adversary after the collapse of the Soviet Union. For years the idea of a conflict of cultures did indeed appear bizarre and a pure fabrication until, in 2001, a handful of Arabs brought down the World Trade Center with hijacked aircraft. So, lo and behold, the USA had its longed-for new war, prophesied by soothsayer Huntington from out of that centre of American banks and secret services – the Council on Foreign Relations which might suitably be re-named the 'Council on Foreign Invasions'. This was the war on (supposedly Islamist) terror which it might well be practical to launch against about sixty countries that supposedly gave shelter to terrorists or otherwise armed or supported them. Not including, of course, the United States – although none other than the United States had trained and employed legions of Islamic terrorists (including a certain Osama bin Laden) at a time when there was the matter of throwing the Soviet Union out of Afghanistan with the help of 'fundamentalists', because (as we now know) the USA itself wanted to go there.

We thus see that the Council is nothing other than the geo-strategic think-tank of the USA where future global developments are anticipated — and where of course know-how and personnel are available who then prepare and set in train such desired developments. The Council is actually the brain of the USA, where the States give their thoughts free rein and link them to the overall leadership apparatus. So 'Relations' is actually a euphemism for strategies, with strategies in the USA being a further euphemism for exploitation, oppression and 'invasion'.

The Bilderbergers are the European conveyor belt for the almost entirely American 'Council'. The 'American third' of Bilderberg membership is recruited almost entirely from 'Council' personnel, so that such members can be used to attune Europe to the American way of thinking. The Council on Foreign Relations is, moreover, regarded as being under Jesuit influence. Several leading 'Council' members have links with the Jesuits or were educated at Jesuit establishments, for example former American Secretary of State Madeleine Albright, long-time NBC anchorman Tom Brokaw, and well-known physicist Shirley Jackson.

# The world's greatest locust

Henry R. Kravis is one of the most notorious 'locusts' in the United States. Together with a certain George R. Roberts and a certain Jerome Kohlberg (who is, by the way, another philanthropist) he had been a partner of the investment bank Bear Stearns which collapsed in 2008. In 1976, these three went independent as the investment company Kohlberg, Kravis, Roberts & Co. Their speciality was leveraged buyouts. Normally the debt for a purchase fell to none other than the purchased company itself, i.e. capital was borrowed and then offered as security for the purchased company. So after the purchase the company in question was often very much in debt and had to work off its own purchase. At the same time, or alternatively, the company was broken up so that the expensive borrowed finance could be paid back out of the proceeds from selling (all) parts of the company, and then under the line the sale of the separate parts could generate a profit. A profit was also made possible by the so-called leverage effect: when the income return on the total capital was higher than the interest for the borrowed capital. This led to a higher return on the (often low) own capital. Companies were regarded as nothing more than tradable goods, to be bought cheaply using borrowed money in order to make a profit out of the sale of the various parts, which often did the company no good. In 1988 journalists Bryan Burrough and John Helyar wrote a book about Kohlberg, Kravis, Roberts & Co's most spectacular purchase. It was about the battle between Kohlberg, Kravis and other bidders for the takeover of the American grocery giant RJR Nabisco (formerly National Biscuit Company). The bidding contest threatened to create an ever higher purchase price and thus ever higher indebtedness for RJR Nabisco. The book's title was *Barbarians at the Gate – The Fall of RJR Nabisco*. The American business journal *The Economist* caricatured Kravis's investment company KKR as 'KKRackers'.

Henry R. Kravis is right at the top of the tree in the USA. He is a member of the Board of Directors of the Council on Foreign Relations where other resonant names are also to be found: Richard E. Salomon (investment banker and Rockefeller adviser), Kenneth M. Duberstein (Ronald Reagan's Chief of Staff), Martin S. Feldstein (an economic adviser to Ronald Reagan), Stephen Friedman (former Goldman Sachs director and Bush adviser), David M. Rubenstein (Director of one of the largest investment companies in the world, the Carlyle Group, which likes to invest in the wars plotted by whichever government is in power).

# The bustling professor

According to a biographical profile in *Business Week*, Victor Halberstadt is an economics professor at Leiden University in Holland, the very town in which the Bilderberg office resides. But that is perhaps merely a sideline. *Business Week* also remarks: 'This man has links with 42 executive groups, directorates and boards of directors distributed across six different industries.' A genuine Bilderberg type indeed. Networking is everything. In this respect the above estimate of a maximum of 24 postings per Bilderberger was thoroughly naïve. It explains why Halberstadt is a professor only to a small extent, while being on the other hand a powerful player. Among the firms he takes part in directing are the American investment bank Goldman Sachs and – can you believe it? – Daimler and (at times) DaimlerChrysler. Yet again this shows that the DaimlerChrysler 'world enterprise' must have been a top undertaking among the Bilderbergers. (See chapter: The 'Global Enterprise')

# A strategist for Europe

Étienne Davignon, one of the most important Bilderberg leaders, attended the oldest, still existing, Catholic university in the world, the Catholic University of Leuven, Belgium. After graduating as a Doctor of Law at the end of the 1950s, Davignon rose to become a central figure in European industry and politics and one of the most important strategists of the European Union. Having first been Belgium's Foreign Minister, he then became (from 1974 to 1977) the first head of the International Energy Agency (IEA). Thereafter he became a member of the European Commission which he headed as Vice President from 1981 to 1985. In 1989 he joined the Board of Directors at the large Belgian bank Société Générale de Belgique (SGB) and in addition directed (with others) numerous large enterprises such as the Belgian mining concern Union Min-ière, the energy supplier Tractabel, the German chemical giant BASF, the US pharmaceutical enterprise Gilead (developer of the anti-flu drug Tamiflu), the powerful waste-water treatment firm Suez, the Luxembourg steel concern Arbed and the Italian car manufacturer Fiat. Davignon played an important role in numerous European think-tanks, e.g. the European Round Table of Indus-trialists and the Friends of Europe. European politics and European business have scarcely ever been as closely knit as they were through Davignon. In 1991 he became President of the Association pour l'union monétaire de l'Europe (Association for the Monetary Union of Europe). Among the Bilderbergers this strategist for Europe occupied a seat on their so-called 'steering committee', and subsequently became honorary president of the gathering.

# The 'godfather'

Here we have the man who was first named by our likable hotel director as the leader of the pack: Henry Kissinger. So who or what is Henry Kissinger? Wikipedia calls him an historian. Well, that is of course one way of describing him. As a leading member of the Council on Foreign Relations he has been stirring the pot of our planet's history for so long that it's hard to imagine things without him. For the more elderly among us, who remember Kissinger's most effective phase during the 1970s, he is quite simply a shining light or, you could say, a dove of peace. He brought peace wherever he went, on the water, on the land, and in the air. For a while it was not easy to retain an overview of what he was doing.

But let's take things one after the other. We hear that Kissinger brought about détente between East and West and also introduced the peace talks between North and South Vietnam, for which he was immediately awarded the Nobel Peace Prize. He is even supposed to have brought about a peaceful conclusion to the October 1973 Yom-Kippur war between Egypt, Syria and Israel. Almost too good to be true. American star journalist Seymour Hersh, who has frequently uncovered dubious affairs in American politics, thought so too. For him Kissinger the messenger of peace is, in fact, the angel of death who is responsible for the bombardment of civilians in Vietnam. 'When the rest of us can't sleep we count sheep, and this guy has to count burned and maimed Cambodian and Vietnamese babies until the end of his life.'[30] 'Globalization is simply another expression for US domination', said the boss of the Bilderbergers.[31]

In 2001 the well-known American journalist Christopher Hitchens enumerated Kissinger's probable crimes in his book *The Trial of Henry Kissinger*.

In 1973 (incidentally on 11 September), when he was already

flapping about in the world as the inevitable dove of peace (having for a long while already been genteelly gossiping with the Bilderbergers), he contrived with the CIA to set in train a bloody putsch against the democratically-elected President of Chile, Salvador Allende, who did not survive. And neither did Chilean democracy. The putsch led to the bloody dictatorship of Augusto Pinochet, who had objectors tortured to death in concentration camps or simply thrown out of helicopters into the sea. Saddam Hussein is an innocent lamb by comparison. Over a million (presumed) 'left-wingers' had to leave the country and were granted asylum by Sweden where Olof Palme (who was later assassinated) was in charge. Over 28,000 people were brutally tortured during Pinochet's dictatorship. On 10 September 2001, the family of the Chilean general René Schneider, who had been murdered in 1970, brought an action in the Federal High Court against Kissinger and the former CIA boss Richard Helms because they said the order to murder Schneider had come directly from Kissinger. (*Sydney Morning Herald*, 30.4.2002, inter alia) One day later, on 11 September 2001, the 28th anniversary of the Pinochet putsch, the Chilean human rights organization lodged an accusation against Kissinger and others on account of their presumed involvement in Operation Condor in which several Latin American dictatorships had joined forces to pursue and assassinate regime critics. News of this was somewhat overshadowed owing to this being the day when the twin towers of the World Trade Center were blown up by unknown perpetrators.

On account of a variety of actions concerning presumed war crimes having been lodged, there were from time to time a number of countries to which dove of peace Kissinger was unable to travel. For example human rights activists and affected parties accuse him of having had his finger in the pie of the bloody invasion of East Timor in 1975 and 1976 during which unverified reports claim that 200,000 people lost their lives. Rumours and strange coincidences even link Kissinger to the death of Aldo Moro who was head of the

Italian Christian Democrats (Democrazia Cristiana, DC) in 1978. In the eyes of the Americans, Moro was intending to commit a felony worthy of death, namely to form a government in collaboration with Italy's Communist Party (the so-called 'Historic Compromise').

Moro's offer of openness towards the left 'was met in the USA by bitter opposition which culminated in actual murder threats towards the DC politicians', wrote historian and publicist Gerhard Feldbauer. When Moro visited Washington he 'had been subjected to massive pressure'. The Secretary of State and 'covert US President' at the time was Henry Kissinger. In Chile they did 'what the United States does in order to defend its interests in other countries'. That was what 'Kissinger's President', Gerald Ford, had warned the Italians. Eleonora Moro, the murdered DC leader's widow, Feldbauer reported, had said 'that during his state visit her husband had been threatened with massive consequences if he did not end his collaboration with the communists'. 'Either you stop, or it will cost you dear', a man who had not been named by her husband had warned. 'Her husband had taken this so seriously that on his return to Rome he had drawn up his will.'

Kissinger followed 'hard on Moro's heels' when he returned to Italy. In an interview he had stated bluntly that the task of the CIA was 'to create realities'. A correspondent close to the CIA had interpreted this in the *New York Times* to mean that he was virtually certain that the confused situation in Italy would be resolved by the secret activities of the CIA. In subsequent years Kissinger's attacks on Moro had grown 'even more biting', wrote Feldbauer. He had called him 'Italy's Allende' – which must surely be understood as a powerful threat.[32] On 16 March 1978 Aldo Moro was kidnapped by the CIA unit 'Red Brigades' and murdered after being held hostage for 55 days. As far as I can see, this is the only 'evidence of a link' between Kissinger and the case of Moro's murder. There are no robust proofs, so the matter of Kissinger's role in the 'case of Moro' must be accompanied by a large question mark.

# The embarrassing prince

Ever since Prince Ernst August of Hanover was alleged to have publicly urinated at the Hanover Expo, we have known that princes can be rather embarrassing. However, by comparison with Prince Bernhard of the Netherlands, that scandal-laden founder of the Bilderbergers, Ernst August is a mere nonentity.

Prince Bernhard had the idea of setting up the Bilderberg group in 1954 as a 'conference for the promotion of understanding' between the USA and Europe – or so he said. We have already described how it actually came about. Whatever the case may be, though, the fact is that he was a rather dubious founding father. 'On account of his liking for the Nazis, his sexual peccadillos and his grubby dealings with big business, the man with the carnation in his buttonhole was a permanent source of trouble for the House of Orange', wrote *Der Spiegel* on 6 December 2004.

The business career of Prince Bernhard zur Lippe-Biesterfeld (as he was still known at the time) began in 1935 with I.G. Farben, which was for a while the fourth-largest business in the world and which had connections with, among others, Rockefeller's Standard Oil. 'Prince Bernhard always denied having had a liking for National Socialism. As a young man, however, he had been a member of the Mounted SS, the SA Flying Squadron and the NS Motorised Corps', we read on the website of the TV broadcaster Phoenix (Kai Klauder, PHOENIXonline). In the middle of the 1930s Prince zur Lippe-Biesterfeld became acquainted with Princess Juliana, daughter of Queen Wilhelmina of the Netherlands, and they were married on 7 January 1937. Although prior to the wedding he had resigned from all National Socialist organizations, his first trip abroad as a member of the Dutch royal family is said to have been a visit to Hitler of all people. In 1938 his daughter Beatrix was born, until 2013 Queen of the Netherlands and his successor with the Bilderbergers.

During World War II, Bernhard fled to London where he sought employment with the British secret service, for which Retinger was also working. A biography by the Dutch journalist Philip Dröge (*Beroep: Meesterspion, het geheime leven van prins Bernhard*, Amsterdam 2003; 'Profession: master spy – the secret life of Prince Bernhard') describes Bilderberger founder Bernhard as a 'master spy' with a 'secret life' during World War II and thereafter. *Der Spiegel* of 1 July 2002: 'According to the author's researches in Washington, London and Berlin, the noble gentleman is thought to have spied for at least eight secret services including those of America, Poland and Britain, and also for German intelligence under Admiral Canaris.' Well, well! However, *Der Spiegel* remarks further that 'Dutch historians' had criticized the book: 'The designation of master spy was "too much of an honour for Prince Bernhard".' Aha, and why? 'Proven is only the fact that Prince Bernhard was acquainted with spies of every shade.' Well, surely a man who is acquainted with 'spies of every shade' is nothing other than a master spy? No ordinary agent would have had such kudos.

After the war, 'Agent Orange' (Prince Bernhard's nickname referring to the House of Orange into which he had married), who is also said to have had contacts in the American mafia, cashed in to the tune of 1.1 million dollars of palm grease from American Lockheed for the purchase of the scandalous aircraft Lockheed F-104 'Starfighter' for the Dutch air-force. Confronted by Prime Minister Joop den Uyl with the choice either of facing prosecution or of withdrawing from all his posts, Bernhard chose the latter option.

One factor which contributed to making Prince Bernhard interesting for the Bilderbergers was the participation of the Dutch royal family in the largest concern in the world, Royal Dutch Shell. Even in those days the enterprise was among the world's largest, and in 2008, with its turnover of 458 milliard dollars, it was definitely the largest on the globe. It was thought that the Dutch royals used to hold 25 per cent in the company, but nowadays their holding is said to be less. Nevertheless, Prince Bernhard (and later his daughter Beatrix) still count amongst the most powerful. In today's world there are few who are as mighty as the oil companies without which nothing in today's world would be able to function, not even those much-praised electrical cars, for they, too, need greasing, and the electricity they use has to be produced somewhere, usually by an oil-fired power plant. In 1988 Prince Bernhard donated the proceeds from the sale of two paintings from his private collection to the World Wildlife Fund. However, the Fund returned most of this to the Prince to enable him, so it is said, to fund a team combating the illegal ivory trade. That team really did exist, but instead of combating the trade it allegedly joined the illegal ivory business (see PHOENIX Online). Prince Bernhard died in 2004, exactly fifty years after the founding of the Bilderbergers.

# The oil princess

Queen Beatrix of the Netherlands, born in 1938, is the daughter of the first Bilderberg chairman, Prince Bernhard of the Netherlands. She studied sociology, law and business management at Leiden, where Bilderberg boss Victor Halberstadt teaches economics and also where the Bilderberg office is located. In 2005 she was awarded an honorary doctorate by the University of Leiden.

Dutch queens have long been counted among the richest women in the world. The value of Queen Beatrix's fortune is estimated to amount to 5.5 milliard dollars. More important than this, however, is the fact that as a shareholder she participates in managing the fortunes of Royal Dutch Shell. Shell is prominently represented among the Bilderbergers. In addition to Queen Beatrix the following have been among its representatives at the conferences:

— John Kerr, Director of Shell Transport and Trading Company Plc, later Royal Dutch Shell Plc,
— Jeroen van der Veer, Chairman of Royal Dutch Shell Group, later Chairman of Royal Dutch Shell Plc,
— Jorma Ollila, Chairman of Royal Dutch Shell Plc,
— Cornelius A.J. Herkströter, Chairman of the Board of Royal Dutch/Shell Group.

In 2005, Shell representatives among the Bilderbergers were also able to meet Angela Merkel, at the time Chair of the Christian Democratic Union (CDU), and soon to become German Chancellor. In 2009 the CDU released a promotional film that resembled a scarcely-camouflaged Shell advert, when watched with the sound switched off: A young man is driving through the dusk searching for a filling station. All around him Shell's colours, yellow and red, shine out. Several times — somewhat out of focus — the Shell logo also appears in the background. Anyone who knows how promotional films are planned and designed will find it hard to believe that this was a coincidence.

Since the early 1990s, Royal Dutch Shell has been labouring under a full-blown scandal, namely the reported utterly heedless exploitation of Ogoni homelands in Nigeria's Niger Delta. 'The list of accusations against Shell is long', alleged faz.net on 9 June 2009: 'The company participated in countless human rights abuses, including the torture and execution of Ogoni people by the military regime of the day. And Shell would also have to take responsibility for serious environmental damage in the Niger Delta.'

The battle of the Ogoni against the Nigerian government and the Bilderberger oil-multinational finally led in 1995 to the execution of the leader of the rebellion and winner of the Alternative Nobel Prize, Ken Saro-Wiwa, and eight of his co-revolutionaries. Shortly before his death, Saro-Wiwa had written his book *A Month and a Day* (1995) about the battle of the Ogoni people against Shell. In 1996 his bereaved family brought an action against Shell: 'They accused the oil company of helping the junta to silence its opponents, or at least of quietly tolerating the crackdown. The oil company had always denied this energetically as being "false and unfounded", claiming it had demanded that the regime should exercise clemency.'

On 8 June 2009 the plaintiffs and the company agreed on a compensation payment of 15.5 million dollars. However, Shell denied any responsibility for the executions and described the payment as 'a humanitarian gesture' while also recognizing that 'the Ogoni people had suffered'. (faz.net)

# The 'prince of darkness' . . .

. . . has been involved with the Bilderbergers annually since 2001. His real name is Richard Perle. Perle is one of the leading Neo-conservatives, strategic planners and war-mongers of the USA who backed not only first-strikes, which contravene international law, and also preventive strikes; in short, bilateral or multilateral attacks. The club law of the stronger is what counts for him in international politics, and he makes no great effort to disguise this. He simply tells the truth and nothing but the truth. In an interview with the Public Broadcasting System (PBS) on 14 November 2002, for example, he declared:

> The lesson of history is that democracies don't initiate wars of aggression, and if we want to live in a peaceful world, then there's very little we can do to bring that about [that is] more effective than promoting a democracy. People who live in democratic societies don't like to pay for massive military machines. Democratic societies don't empower their executives to make unilateral decisions to plunge countries into war. Wars have been started by tyrants who have complete control and who can squander the resources of their people to build up military machines.

The only conclusion one can draw from this must be that the USA is no longer a democratic society. Firstly the population is groaning under the weight of a parasitic military-industrial complex, and secondly since 2001 the USA has launched surprise attacks on two countries in contravention of international law. Furthermore, this means that George W. Bush, in whose administration Perle played a leading role, must have been one of those very tyrants. Bilderberger Richard Perle is a member of several, let's say 'strategic', think-tanks, including the Council on Foreign Relations (CFR) and the Project for a New American Century (PNAC). The PNAC is regarded as the core of the Neoconservative, or Neocon, movement. This is where the wars against Afghanistan and Iraq were being considered long before 11 September 2001. (And let's not forget that a new catastrophe, after the pattern of Japan's surprise attack on Pearl Harbor in 1941, might well have brought those desired events forward.) The 'new American century' certainly began punctually during its very first year, on 11 September 2001. The attacks on the twin towers were the hotly-desired justification for those journeys to Afghanistan and Iraq. The PNAC, as the guiding spirit behind the post 9/11 wars, is an especially aggressive hornets' nest of the Council on Foreign Relations.

# Kosher Nostra . . .

. . . is, according to *Der Spiegel*, a nickname for Paul Wolfowitz, the next Neocon and darkly obscure Bilderberg strategist. Having initially been Deputy Defence Secretary under Bush, Wolfowitz is seen 'as a pioneer of the new world order' and as 'the mastermind and puppet-master' of the Iraq war, wrote *Der Stern* with unusual frankness on its website on 15 April 2003. Wolfowitz was 'strongly pro-Israel' and, 'as the chief strategist of the Bush administration', he had 'succeeded in furthering his vision of American supremacy'. Active like Perle in the CFR and the PNAC, he, too, waffles on about democracy and liberation: 'We came not as occupiers but as liberators. We will not stay a single day longer than necessary.' This is indeed perfectly correct, since he means so long as people like Wolfowitz determine what is meant by 'necessary'. Bush's cowboy behaviour and the way he thinks in black-and-white terms are attributable, not least, to Wolfowitz. 'Our friends', he wrote, 'will be protected, and our enemies punished. And those who withhold their support will regret their actions'. (Website of *Der Stern*) The Neocons' internal journal *The Weekly Standard* reacted by recommending George W. Bush for the Nobel Peace Prize. A joke? Of course not: remember Kissinger. (And, more recently, remember also Obama.) *Der Stern* has stated that Wolfowitz needed '9/11' for his unparalleled career. 'It was those attacks which made him what he is today – unquestionably the most influential Deputy Defence Secretary in the history of the USA.' Which sounds almost as though those attacks were instigated by Wolfowitz himself.

Just like his boss, Defence Secretary and Bilderberger Donald Rumsfeld, Wolfowitz eventually became untenable for the Bush administration. So in 2005 he was fawningly complimented into the post of World Bank President – as successor to Bilderberger James

David Wolfensohn (see below). A joke. 'How can the World Bank hand out recommendations about good governance when its President broke international law by invading Iraq?', a Mexican critic was quoted as saying in the minutes of a meeting of the Bank (according to *Spiegel Online*, 12.4.2007). And the nomination of Bilderberger Wolfowitz as successor to Bilderberger Wolfensohn did then indeed turn into a farce. It signifies nothing other than that global elites provide one another with jobs and sinecures without any account being taken of their qualifications or suitability (e.g. character). For example Wolfowitz's girlfriend Shaha Riza worked for the World Bank. But since the World Bank doesn't countenance such relationships among its employees, Riza was moved to another property of the global elite – the US State Department. Of course her move to the State Department was sweetened by a promotion and a raise in annual salary. (See *Spiegel Online*, 12.4.2007)

But Bilderberger Wolfowitz proved to be too much in the long run even for the World Bank. Only two years later, in June 2007, he had to leave again, making his tenure as President of the World Bank one of the shortest since World Bank Presidents have existed. His successor was Bilderberger Robert B. Zoellick.

# Rummy the Neocon

Donald Rumsfeld, leading Neocon and strategist in the Iraq and Afghanistan wars and also member of CFR and PNAC, was Bush's Defence Secretary for a long period. He, too, earned his stripes not only because of the wars but also as a shareholder of the pharma enterprise Gilead Sciences, inventors of the reportedly anti-influenza drug Tamiflu, because UNO was constantly busy stirring up panics about a putative influenza epidemic. For many millions of dollars, the drug was purchased 'prophylactically' by countless countries. Every new global 'flu panic stirred up by the World Health Organization, and disseminated by the media companies already mentioned, provides pure PR for 'Rummy' and his pills. If we're not careful we, too, will one day be forced to swallow the stuff.

# Wolfensohn, son of a wolf

Bilderberger James David Wolfensohn was Paul Wolfowitz's predecessor in the post of World Bank President. He was nominated for this post by US President and CFR member Bill Clinton, who had himself also been a guest of the Bilderbergers in 1991, before being elected President of the USA. Unlike Wolfowitz, Wolfensohn was President of the World Bank for ten years (from 1995 to 2005). CFR member Wolfensohn is a well-trained and experienced banker whose career has taken him through the jewels of the international banking scene, including J. Henry Schroder's investment bank and Salomon Brothers. In the 1980s he had founded his own investment company, together with the subsequent Bilderberger and former boss of the USA's Federal Reserve Bank, Paul A. Volcker. Wolfensohn furthermore belongs to various think-tanks and institutions in which other Bilderbergers also participate, for example the Rockefeller Foundation (which sports a globe in its logo).

# The proprietors of Sweden

The von Wallenberg banking dynasty can look back over an impressive family tree of bishops, officers, bankers and industrialists. 'The Wallenberg clan with its Swedish commercial empire has long been legendary', wrote faz.net on 16 September 2006. 'Its enterprises were active globally before the word "globalization" had even been coined. The power and influence of the Wallenbergs unfolded quietly and steadily over the course of the twentieth century ... The Wallenbergs have been a central component of Swedish commercial history for 150 years.'

It is said that the clan owns shares in over 140 enterprises worldwide. And in Sweden it is involved in all the important companies such as Ericsson (telecommunications), Astra Zeneca (pharmaceuticals), Stora Enso (paper), Atlas Copco (mechanical engineering), SAS (aviation), Electrolux (household appliances), SEB (banking). And Jacob Wallenberg is a member of the international advisory group of the Council on Foreign Relations.

The above brief considerations about the main Bilderbergers will serve to show that those who have the strongest voice are the bankers and the industrialists. However, that is in no way a complete account of the Bilderberg network. Several thousand other heavyweights had already met one another at Bilderberg gatherings. The lists of members and guests read like a *Who's Who* of the western world. An analysis of this network would require a work comprising several volumes and would greatly resemble an encyclopaedia of the world's rich and powerful.

But where, in all this, can we find the notorious US President George W. Bush? Well, as we have already indicated, Bilderberg meetings are attended only by important people – the ringmasters...

# The gerontocrats

One mustn't fail to mention that leadership of the Bilderbergers is up against a serious problem: old age. Above all the bellwether himself has a good many years behind him. David Rockefeller is almost 100 (99), Henry Kissinger 91, Victor Halberstadt is about 75, Étienne Davignon and James Wolfensohn are 81, Donald Rumsfeld 82, Henry R. Kravis, 70, and Richard Perle, 73, are among the youngsters. The only truly important woman is Queen Beatrix of the Netherlands, who abdicated on 30.4.2013 in favour of her son, Willem-Alexander. (As of April 2014) Here are the birth dates of the most important conference participants:

> David Rockefeller Sr. * 12 June 1915
> Henry Alfred Kissinger * 27 May 1923
> Henry R. Kravis * 6 January 1944
> Victor Halberstadt * 1939
> Vicomte Étienne Davignon * 4 October 1932
> Beatrix Wilhelmina Armgard * 31 January 1938
> Richard Norman Perle * 16 September 1941
> James David Wolfensohn KBE, AO * 1 December 1933
> Donald Henry Rumsfeld * 9 July 1932
> Paul Dundes Wolfowitz * 22 December 1943

For many decades the same personages have indeed led and put their stamp on the Bilderbergers. And indeed the Bilderbergers are thus a gerontocracy. Normally a gerontocracy can be described as being petrified or fossilized, so do the Bilderbergers truly intend to live and die with these people? We can certainly allow ourselves to be agog as to what will happen when Kissinger, Rockefeller, Halberstadt and Davignon shuffle off this mortal coil. Although global elites normally think and act dynastically, it is hard to discover many Kissinger or Rockefeller successors at the Bilderberg Conferences. Or to ask the opposite question: Would these elderly gents still find it necessary at the age of 85 or nearly 100 to jet around the world in order to attend Bilderberg and other conferences if a 'useful' rising generation existed? Or is this great power game their only elixir of life?

# The Israel Lobby

'The *New York Times*, the *Financial Times*, the *New York Review of Books*, the *Chicago Tribune*, the *New York Observer*, the *National Interest* and *The Nation* all published respectful comments', we read in a 2006 article of this title which preceded the publication in 2007 of the book *The Israel Lobby and U.S. Foreign Policy* by the two American scholars John J. Mearsheimer and Stephen M. Walt about the role of those who represent the interests of Israel in American politics. 'Some positive reactions even came from Israel', the article continues. At great personal risk (for example the danger of being accused of 'anti-Semitism'), Mearsheimer and Walt have pushed open a door, and it would be fatal not to step through it. Their intention was not to stoke up a new wave of anti-Semitism, as the Israel lobby constantly wants to make us believe, but to help us arrive at last at a realistic and unvarnished view of the state of Israel, of its interests and of its influence in the world, and thus also of the possibility of treating the country as an equal and of attaining the impartiality which alone can help us analyse the strategies of states and interest groups.

Mearsheimer and Walt discuss the insidious undermining of the American state by the Israel Lobby. Well, the Israel Lobby also appears at Bilderberg Conferences under the guise of the USA. Wherever leading echelons of the USA are at work, they are to a great extent influenced by the Israel Lobby, and this fact should on no account be ignored in the context of the Bilderbergers.

## Henry Kissinger

Let us consider Henry Kissinger, who is a leading light and 'god-father' of the Bilderbergers, and at the same time a prominent representative of the Israel Lobby. Mearsheimer and Walt pay detailed attention to his role as Secretary of State in Nixon's administration. In reality, he was its covert president. So why didn't Kissinger himself become President? Quite simply: only 'natural born Americans' can be President, and Kissinger was born at Fürth in Germany on 27 May 1923 and did not attain American citizenship until 19 June 1943.

Mearsheimer and Walt describe the benevolent support given to Israel by the Kissinger-Nixon administration in times of war, for instance during the war with Egypt from 1968 to 1970. 'Although the Nixon Administration did not give Israel all the weapons it asked for, which occasionally led to sharp exchanges between the two governments, the United States did provide increased arms supplies... A memorandum of understanding in 1972 committed the United States to provide planes and tanks on a long-term basis.'[33]

They say that Nixon and Kissinger promised to consult Israel before entering into new peace negotiations, which amounted to a superpower granting a tiny country the right to a veto. According to Near-East expert William Quandt, 'the United States Near East policy consisted in little more than open support for Israel'. And in the opinion of Israel's Foreign Minister, Abba Eban, this was the golden era of US weapons supplies to Israel.[34]

However, they continue, Kissinger's support for Israel went way beyond the supply of armaments. On some occasions the American Secretary of State became a full emissary of Israel, for example during the 1973 Yom Kippur War.

During the armistice negotiations, especially in the talks with the Soviet leadership, the authors describe Kissinger as taking care to ensure the continuation of Israel's freedom to act. In doing this he utterly ignored President Nixon's wishes. Nixon had in fact instructed him to tell Soviet General Secretary Brezhnev that the USA wanted to use the war to attain comprehensive peace in the Near East. In contradiction to this, Kissinger succeeded in bringing about a standstill in which Israel retained the upper hand. Records show that in Moscow Kissinger had on several occasions represented Israel's interests 'very much in contradiction to Nixon's wishes'.

Mearsheimer and Walt repeatedly quote evidence of how the US Secretary of State actually stood up for Israel. For instance, to enable it to improve its position he permitted Israel to disregard a UN resolution demanding a cessation of hostilities within twelve hours. In fact, the American Secretary of State developed an astonishingly independent life of his own in the way he assumed presidential powers and competencies. One gains the impression that Bilderberger Kissinger had always been not only a global operator but also a Trojan horse for Israel hidden in the upper echelons of the American administration; and also among the Bilderbergers. In 1977, the year of his retirement from the office of Secretary of State, Kissinger became a professor for international diplomacy at the Jesuit Georgetown University in Washington DC. In 1982 he founded the consultancy firm Kissinger Associates. This included Bilderbergers Étienne Davignon, Europe strategist, and Lord Carrington, NATO General Secretary from 1984 to 1988. As one of the directors of the media group Hollinger International (later Sun-Times Media Group), founded by the notorious media tycoon Conrad Black, Kissinger was able to influence public opinion. Worldwide, dozens of newspapers, among others the *Daily Telegraph*, the *Chicago Sun Times*, the *Spectator*, and the *Jerusalem Post*, belonged to Hollinger or Sun-Times. The Sun-Times Media Group went bust in 2009. Among other organizations, Kissinger is a member of the American think-tank Aspen Institute, to which, for example, the German publicist and presenter of ZDF's programme 'heute journal', Claus Kleber, also belongs.

## Paul Wolfowitz

'When Wolfowitz was selected to be deputy defence secretary in January 2001, the *Jerusalem Post* reported that "the Jewish and pro-

Israel communities are jumping for joy",' wrote Mearsheimer and Walt.

'In the spring of 2002', they continue, '*Forward* had pointed out that Wolfowitz was "known as the most hawkishly pro-Israel voice in the Administration" and had in the same year selected him from among fifty important persons as the one who had "consciously pursued Jewish activism".' Furthermore, 'at about the same time, JINSA [the Jewish Institute for National Security Affairs] gave him his Henry M. Jackson Distinguished Service Award for promoting a strong partnership between Israel and the United States, and the *Jerusalem Post*, describing him as "devoutly pro-Israel" had named him as its "Man of the Year" in 2003.'[35]

Mearsheimer and Walt also tell us that Wolfowitz was the foremost anti-Iraq warmonger not only before but also immediately after the attack on the World Trade Center.

Important though the Neocons had been in scheming towards war with Iraq, they would have failed to persuade either Clinton or Bush to invade had it not been for the 9/11 attack in 2001. September 11 provided the turning point, say the authors, quoting Robert Kagan, policy adviser to the Neocons. Bush was suddenly no longer the same man. And the Neocons, including Wolfowitz and others, had played an important part in persuading both the President and the Vice President that war was now the right thing. September 11 was 'the new context' into which the Neocons could embed all their old ideas about US foreign policy. At the very moment when the administration were trying their best to get to grips with a unique catastrophe, the Neocons, according to Kagan, had been able to bring their 'ready-made concept of the world' out of the closet. Wolfowitz especially had been pressing for a war against Iraq. At a meeting with Bush as early on as 15 September he had spoken up for an attack on Iraq even though there had been no proof of any involvement by Iraq in the attacks. According to a Republican present at the meeting, Wolfowitz had brought up Iraq repeatedly, 'like a parrot', so that after a while he began to get on the

President's nerves. This also accorded with the line followed by the Jewish Institute for National Security Affairs. According to Mearsheimer and Walt, the Institute had released a declaration on 13 September 2001 stating: 'A long investigation to prove Osama bin Laden's guilt with prosecutorial certainty is entirely unnecessary. He is guilty in word and deed. His history is the source of his culpability. The same holds true for Saddam Hussein.'[36]

A curious proof indeed of someone's guilt.

### Richard Perle

During Paul Wolfowitz's period as Deputy Defence Secretary in the Bush administration, Bilderberger Richard Perle, together with Henry Kissinger, was on the US Defence Policy Board Advisory Committee, a strategic group advising Secretary Donald Rumsfeld, who himself was also a PNAC member and Bilderberger. Perle is a member of numerous ultra-rightwing think-tanks including the JINSA mentioned earlier. Like Kissinger, Perle also occupied a leading position in the Hollinger media group (later Sun-Times Media Group). And he was also active not only with the Bilderbergers but also in PNAC, that centre of ultra-rightwing warmongering in the USA. Even before 9/11 PNAC were putting pressure on the American administration to begin the very wars on which the USA did then embark after 9/11. The question we must ask is: Was that really in the interests of the USA or was it rather in the interests of another country entirely? Both Iraq and Iran are located more or less close to Israel but not to the United States. Whereas Israel may have been able to claim a subjective sense of being threatened by those two countries, the threat to the United States from Iraq conjured up by President George W. Bush was utterly absurd.

Mearsheimer and Walt also mention that as early on as 1996, together with David Wurmser and Douglas Feith, Perle had authored 'the famous "Clean Break" report' which recommended to the Israeli Prime Minister Netanyahu that he 'should concentrate on disempowering Saddam in Iraq — an important strategic goal for Israel' — and also take steps to bring about a new order in the whole of the Near East. These are the steps then undertaken by the USA after 11 September 2001. Even a columnist on the Israeli newspaper *Haaretz* 'warned Feith and Perle, they "are walking a fine line between their loyalty to American governments ... and Israeli interests".'[37]

This shows that in matters concerning the United States the tail had long since been wagging the dog. The relationship between Israel and the USA can best be described as resembling the connection between a brain and its muscle-bound body. The work of the Israel Lobby has led to policies, and above all to wars, that have done great harm to the USA. Although hitherto it would not have been possible for anyone to harm the USA, one may now wonder whether this subjection to others might be the very thing which in the end could lead to the destruction of the American nation.

# Part 4

# A GERMAN MAFIA?

# The silence of the Bilderbergers

After investigating the background of the Bilderbergers I came to the conclusion that they should not simply be left entrenched behind their silence. I briefly considered consulting an adviser on religious sects since basically, like the Jesuits' vows of poverty and chastity, which have a distinctly religious element, the silence of the Bilderbergers might be seen to resemble a 'vow of silence'.

If journalists cannot be granted access, then it ought to be possible at least to ask what the members of this peculiar 'unification church' get up to. So I filtered from my database of official Bilderbergers all the German participants of the past eighteen years, which resulted in an imposing list:

| | |
|---|---|
| Ackermann, Josef | Lauk, Kurt J. |
| Bertram, Christoph | Merkel, Angela |
| Burda, Hubert | Mosdorf, Siegmar |
| Cromme, Gerhard | Nass, Matthias |
| Döpfner, Mathias | Perger, Werner A. |
| Engelen-Kefer, Ursula | Perthes, Volker |
| Fischer, Joschka | Pflüger, Friedbert |
| Haussmann, Helmut | Polenz, Ruprecht |
| Ischinger, Wolfgang | Reitzle, Wolfgang |
| Issing, H. C. Otmar | Rühe, Volker |
| Joffe, Josef | Sandschneider, Eberhard |
| Kastrup, Dieter | Scharping, Rudolf |
| Keitel, Hans Peter | Schäuble, Wolfgang |
| Klaeden, Eckart von | Schily, Otto |
| Kleinfeld, Klaus | Schrempp, Jürgen E. |
| Kopper, Hilmar | Schulz, Ekkehard D. |
| Lamers, Karl A. | Sommer, Theo |

| | |
|---|---|
| Späth, Lothar | Weber, Jürgen |
| Strube, Jürgen | Westerwelle, Guido |
| Verheugen, Günter | Wissmann, Matthias |
| Voscherau, Henning | Zumwinkel, Klaus |

In addition, since Kurt Georg Kiesinger all Chancellors of the German Federal Republic are said to have been participants:

| | |
|---|---|
| Kurt Georg Kiesinger | 1957 |
| Willy Brandt | ? |
| Helmut Schmidt | 1973, 1980, 1983, 1986 |
| Helmut Kohl | 1980, 1982, 1988 |
| Gerhard Schröder | 2005 |
| Angela Merkel | 2005 |

*Source (except Brandt): Flegelskamp, Gert: Deutsche Teilnehmer an Bilderberg-Treffen, 16.9.2009, http://www.flegel-g.de/bilderberger-deutsche-01.html*

In view of such a truly incredible assemblage of the German Federal Republic's political and commercial heavyweights, about whose Bilderberg attendance as good as nothing has appeared in the media, I thought it would be quite reasonable to make enquiries as to the meaning and purpose of such an event. I wanted on the one hand to put the Bilderbergers' vow of silence to the test, and on the other, if possible, to learn from the participants a little more about their background.

On 29 April 2009 I therefore composed the following letter:

*Dear . . .*

*I have learned that you have been a participant at the Bilderberg Conferences. As part of a book project on these conferences, undertaken in collaboration with a well-known German publisher, I would like to ask known German participants a few questions. It would be perfectly acceptable for you to remain anonymous if you so wish; please make a note to this effect in your reply.*

*I would ask you to note your answers under the relevant numbers on a separate sheet. You could send these answers by fax or e-mail, or else by post, whichever is most convenient.*

*To enable me to evaluate your reply for purposes of publication, please ensure that I receive it not later than 15 May 2009.*

*With many thanks in anticipation.*

*Kind regards,*
*Gerhard Wisnewski*

I then also set up the following questionnaire, which I posted together with the letter on 30 April 2009 to the German Bilderberg participants about whom I had heard:

1. How are participants at a Bilderberg Conference selected?
2. How and by what means is the invitation presented?
3. What significance does an invitation to a Bilderberg Conference have for a participant?
4. How often and when have you attended a Bilderberg Conference?
5. How would you describe the Bilderberg Conferences?
6. What in your opinion are the Bilderberg Conferences?
7. What in your opinion is the purpose served by the Bilderberg Conferences?
8. Why in your opinion have Bilderberg Conferences been taking place for over fifty years?
9. Are concrete projects discussed and arranged at Bilderberg Conferences? Please kindly quote some examples.
10. Are requests or demands put to the participants?
11. Are participants put under pressure?
12. Have you made any decisions as a consequence of Bilderberg Conferences (example, please)?
13. Is there any conflict of interests between participating at Bilderberg Conferences and your private or public duties? Please give reasons.

14. What relationships arise during or as a result of the conferences?

15. Does a power mechanism arise from these relationships, and how would you describe it?

16. Are the contacts upheld only during a conference or do they persist thereafter?

17. What is the role played by Bilderberg Conferences in your career?

18. To what extent have Bilderberg Conferences been advantageous for your career?

19. To what extent have you been able to obtain professional positions through participating in the conferences?

20. What other advantages has participation brought?

21. Which country do you consider to have the greatest influence at Bilderberg Conferences?

22. Which persons do you consider to have the greatest influence at Bilderberg Conferences, and what is their aim?

23. What role have Bilderberg Conferences played in the formation of commercial alliances and international conglomerates (e.g. DaimlerChrysler)?

24. What role do the Bilderberg Conferences play with regard to so-called 'globalization'?

25. Do you recall some specific experience you have had in relation to the Bilderberg Conferences?

26. Have I forgotten anything else you might like to mention?

I also sent a shorter version of this questionnaire to the former, now quite elderly, German chancellors Helmut Schmidt, Helmut Kohl and Gerhard Schröder.

Initial result: Only one person denied participating at Bilderberg Conferences. This exception was Erwin Teufel, former Minister-President of Baden-Württemberg: 'I am not a member of the Bilderberg Conferences and can therefore not reply to your questions.' My database did indeed show Teufel as an 'unconfirmed member'. So in this respect my Bilderberg 'book-keeping' was correct, and I have removed Teufel from the list. The quality of my database is otherwise upheld by the fact that not a single other person denied participation even after I had, in some cases, written a second time.

Most of those contacted, however, fobbed me off with terse replies.

'Dear Herr Wisnewski', wrote, for instance, a colleague of the President of Deutsche Bank, Josef Ackermann, 'Dr. Ackermann has asked me to thank you for your letter of 29 April in which you informed him about your book project on the Bilderberg Conferences and requested answers to certain questions pertaining to that publication. Dr. Ackermann regrets that it will not be possible for him to reply to your questions.'

No explanation was given as to why it would 'not be possible' for Dr. Ackermann to answer my questions. His hope that his reply would 'meet with my understanding' was in vain since nothing was forthcoming that might have met with 'my understanding'. Was Ackermann's vow of silence the reason, or was the questionnaire too long? Did he have no time, or couldn't he be bothered? Since none of this could be explained there was nothing for me to be understanding about. This boss of a key German enterprise, and master of astronomical monetary values belonging to shareholders, attends the conference of a weird 'unification church' where he wheels and deals regularly with foreign enterprise bosses, top military personnel and secret service bosses. In doing this does he really act in the best interests of those shareholders? I decide to investigate this further in connection with Bilderbergers Schrempp and Zumwinkel as well.

Initially there was no end to the stream of cryptic replies from the Bilderbergers to my questionnaire. The crème de la crème of the Federal Republic's politics and economics continued to bombard me with nebulous letters.

Ackermann's predecessor Hilmar Kopper certainly admitted not only to having 'attended Bilderberg Conferences regularly over many years' and even to having been 'their treasurer' but he, too, hoped for my understanding: 'You will understand that I wish to abide by the Bilderberg ruling that no information is given out about the participants or the content of the conferences.'

Will the shareholders of Deutsche Bank be forthcoming with their understanding? After all, membership of this 'unification church' can coincide with some rather strange enterprise decisions, as we shall see in connection with Schrempp and Zumwinkel.

Meanwhile my reputation as a regular guy, who 'of course understands' everything, continued to hurry on ahead as the Bilderbergers persisted in laying claims on my tolerance. The next to presuppose it was media tycoon Hubert Burda whose wife, Maria Furtwängler, German viewers encounter on their TV screens almost every evening, either in some advert or other or else in an insipid drama or 'whodunit'. Burda's spouse has for some time been amassing prizes including, among others, in 2008, the Jupiter Prize of *Cinema* magazine, which belongs to Hubert Burda's media conglomerate.

'Dear Herr Wisnewski', one of Herr Burda's colleagues was instructed to write, 'Many thanks for your letter to which I am happy to reply. Dr Burda has been invited to attend those conferences from time to time. Since the protocol of the conferences requires them to remain off the record he is unable to answer your questions. He is sure you will understand.'

My experience with Günter Verheugen, Vice-President of the European Commission, i.e. the government of Europe, was similar. He sent an entirely innocuous letter:

'I only attended one of those conferences, and that was at the request of my parliamentary party', he wrote. 'I don't remember exactly when that was, but I do remember where: at the Bürgenstock near Lucerne in Switzerland.'

Well, the Bilderbergers met there twice, in 1981 and in 1995.

I did not gain any specific benefit from the conference, and I subsequently declined invitations until they no longer came. My very limited, one-off experience with the set-up means that I am unable to answer your questions, especially as I cannot remember much about it. I hope you will understand.

What strikes me about this reply is the gingerly way in which EU Commission Vice-President Verheugen refers to the Bilderbergers:

— attendance at the conference was not his own idea,
— he did not 'gain any specific benefit' from it,
— it had been 'a very limited, one-off experience'.

Somehow the feeling I had was of someone trying to give innocuous answers. Either he wants to downplay the true role or the true influence of the Bilderbergers, or — and this possibility should definitely also be considered — he finds the whole thing suspect. Whatever the case may be, Verheugen of Europe would have fitted in very well with the Bilderberg globalists. For fifteen years he was a member of Federal Germany's Foreign Office Committee, and from 1998 to 1999 he was a Minister of State at the Foreign Office under Joschka Fischer, supporter of closer relations between the EU and the USA and also a Bilderberger. In September 1999 he became a member of the EU Commission where he was responsible for the eastward expansion of the EU, a strategic concern for both the EU and the USA. It was high time for the former satellites of the Soviet Union to be tied in with the western hemisphere of influence. On the other hand Verheugen has also been credited with the equally refreshing and true sentence: 'If the EU were to apply for membership in our country, we would be obliged to say: democratically unsatisfactory.'

Quite so. Some are even of the opinion that the EU is turning into a new kind of Soviet Union with a 'pretend parliament' and an out-of-touch government (the Commission). This would doubtless suit the Bilderbergers' bill very well.

One of the next letters brought a moment of relief. For once I was the one being offered understanding: 'I can well understand your journalistic interest in the Bilderberg Conferences', wrote the boss of Axel Springer Verlag, Mathias Döpfner, whose papers on the whole inform everybody about everything – except of course the attendance of their top boss at the Bilderberg Conferences. But that was as far as it went with Döpfner's obliging tone. Just as I had expected, it was then once again my turn to do the understanding. 'I hope you will understand that I am unable to deal with your comprehensive catalogue of questions owing to my numerous obligations elsewhere.'

Might this be true? Or was it rather that Döpfner was *not permitted* to say anything?

Next in the queue came Federal Minister of the Interior, Wolfgang Schäuble. At his behest, a government official hoped I would understand that Herr Schäuble 'is too busy to participate in your book project by answering the questionnaire you have sent'. This sounded almost as though Schäuble thought I was asking him to write the book with me. Would that have gone well? Unlikely. So in the end I was not sorry that, after a long and worried examination of his appointment diary, the Federal Minister of the Interior had found it necessary to decline.

My craving for an original reply had grown exponentially. And, lo and behold, my prayer was answered: 'Participants from the various sections of society, business and science meet regularly at the Bilderberg Conferences', came the information from the office manager of Guido Westerwelle, head of the Free Democratic Party (FDP), although that wasn't actually what I had been wanting to know. I needed replies to my questionnaire. But the letter continued cheerfully: 'In addition to matters of the global economy, it is above all international relationships that are discussed. The approximately 120 participants are selected with a view to achieving a balanced discussion of the various items on the agenda.'

This sounded rather familiar, so I did a bit of googling around the heading 'Bilderberg'. At abgeordnetenwatch.de I found what I was looking for. Here was the generalized and insipid text which Westerwelle had used to fob off concrete questions from a citizen; and not without expressing the hope that 'you will find this helpful'.

> Participants from the various sections of society, business and science meet regularly at the Bilderberg Conferences. In addition to matters of the global economy, it is above all matters of international relationships that are discussed.
>
> The approximately 120 participants are selected with a view to achieving a balanced discussion of the various items on the agenda.

# The rise of Guido W.

Herr Westerwelle's doughty office manager had certainly taken a great deal of trouble on my account by sending me his boss's standard reply in respect of the Bilderbergers. But he had not denied that Westerwelle had attended a conference. Actually there would have been no point in doing so, since Westerwelle certainly did participate in the conference at Istanbul which took place from 31 May to 3 June 2007.

This had made clear to many Bilderberg star-gazers:

— that from 2009 Germany was about to be governed by a black-and-yellow coalition consisting of the Free Democratic Party and the Christian Democratic Union,
— that Westerwelle would occupy the post of a senior minister therein, probably that of Foreign Minister.

It is a fact that, prior to the 2009 Federal elections, both media people and politicians had regarded a black/yellow coalition or else a further Grand Coalition as being the two most likely outcomes. In this connection it is worth once again following the advice of the hotel director mentioned earlier, by examining what became of certain Bilderbergers after a visit to a conference or after their entry into the Bilderberg process. Many politicians and bosses have experienced a steep ascent in their career, right up to the highest offices, after attending a Bilderberg event. Here are a few examples:

| | BB Attendance | Political Post |
|---|---|---|
| K.G. Kiesinger | 1957 | Minister-President of Baden-Württemberg 1958, later Fed. Chancellor |
| Helmut Schmidt | 1973 1st time | Fed. Chancellor from 1974 |
| Helmut Kohl | 1982 1st time 1980 | Fed. Chancellor from 1983 |
| Count Lambsdorff | 1st time 1980 1982 | Toppled the SPD/FDP government in late 1982 |
| Bill Clinton | 1991 | US President from 20.1.1993 |
| Volker Rühe | 1992, previously 1983 and 1991 | Defence Minister from 1992 |
| Tony Blair | 1993 | Labour Party Chair from 1994 |
| J. Schrempp | 1994 1st time | Daimler boss from 24.5.1995 |
| J. Ackermann | 1995 1st time | Deutsche Bank Board from 1996 |
| G. Schröder | 2005 | Orders new elections three weeks after attendance at BB |
| Angela Merkel | 2005 | Fed. Chancellor from Nov. 2005 |
| Guido Westerwelle | 2007 | Vice-Chancellor/Foreign Min. from 2009 |
| Roland Koch | 2009 | Candidate for higher offices from 2009/10 |

All this is purposely formulated 'coincidentally' rather than caus-
ally, for who is to say which came first, the chicken or the egg? After
all, careerists keep on attending one conference or another, whether
before or after any of the many upward steps in their career. So a
conference cannot be regarded as the cause of a step up. Can the
Bilderbergers really be seen as a casting couch for future top politicians and leaders of commerce, as someone once said? Or are they
rather a kind of talent showcase with a nose for upcoming stars?
The fact is that according to surveys the Free Democratic Party
(FDP) was gaining fast even before Westerwelle's attendance at the
Bilderberg Conference, and latest from 2006 onwards it was surpassing one poll-high after another – right until it reached the 18
per cent of votes once striven for by Jürgen Möllemann. Although in
the end the FDP 'only' reached 11 per cent in the 2009 European
elections in Germany, the 'only' calls for quotation marks because
in the 2004 elections their total had been 6.1 per cent. So although
the surveys seemed to show rather exaggerated figures, Westerwelle
and his party have become more vigorous than ever since the Grand
Coalition of SPD and CDU took office. This small party appeared to
profit quite naturally from the miserable plight of the large parties
and the Grand Coalition.

Another factor was added to all this in 2009. This was the election
campaign pursued in rather dilatory fashion by the SPD and Frank-
Walter Steinmeier, their candidate for the chancellorship. (See
Gerhard Wisnewski: *2010. Das andere Jahrbuch. Verheimlicht –
vertuscht – vergessen*, Munich 2009.) It was perfectly obvious that
the SPD's candidate was running only a pretend campaign while
also suffering from a lack of will to win and an acute inhibition with
regard to attacking Federal Chancellor Angela Merkel and the CDU.
Thus the 2009 election campaign posed the question not only as to
what might lie behind the success of the FDP but also what could
have caused the failure of the SPD – for this seemed to be even more
artificial than the rise of the FDP.

And so – purely hypothetically of course – power groups such as the Bilderbergers were in a position to achieve an election success for the FDP in two ways.

Either one could give direct support to the FDP, or one might 'power down' another party (for example with the help of their candidate and the media) to such an extent that voters would more or less be forced to defect to the FDP. The latter would be far less obvious than giving direct support to the desired party.

So the general trend was towards a black/yellow coalition with Westerwelle as Vice Chancellor and probably Foreign Minister. It is unlikely that the Bilderbergers would have failed to notice this — and one would surely have seen nothing wrong with including the future Foreign Minister of the German Federal Republic in one's affairs in advance. Or did things in fact take the opposite course? Was it that the Bilderbergers were actually selecting Westerwelle for higher things? Whatever the case may be, everything went like clockwork. With 14.6 per cent in the election of 2009, the Free Democratic Party attained their best ever result in the history of the Federal Republic. The Social Democratic Party fell by 11.2 per cent since 1998, thus halving their support base of twenty million to ten million. Their candidate for Chancellor, Frank-Walter Steinmeier, looked less and less like a potential Chancellor and more like the grave-digger of German social democracy. A further hint that this might have been the case was that, instead of resigning immediately after the election fiasco, he wanted to continue 'serving' the party as their parliamentary group leader in the Federal Parliament.

# Chancellors by grace of Bilderberger

The lists of Bilderberg attendees also appear to speak for a subordinate role for Steinmeier. Unlike Guido Westerwelle (2007) and Angela Merkel (2005), Steinemeier doesn't appear on any of those lists (and neither, by the way, does Social Democratic Party dissident and top candidate of the left Oskar Lafontaine). So had the Bilderbergers themselves also not chosen Steinmeier to be a future Chancellor? It was certainly a very bad sign. They evidently didn't believe in him. In fact, even when they refrained from direct interference they certainly had a sure instinct for sniffing out up-and-coming individuals. So let's have a look at the other camp. Who from the CDU/CSU Union was among the Bilderbergers' guests in 2009? Once again Angela Merkel, perhaps, just as had been the case prior to her election as Federal Chancellor in 2005?

Not at all. Interestingly it was the Minister-President of Hesse, Roland Koch (CDU), who was invited to the Bilderberg Conference. The very man who, with Merkel, had for some time been talked of as the CDU/CSU Union's candidate for Chancellor. That had been some time ago, however, and I had meanwhile come to believe that none other than Angela Merkel would be the CDU/CSU Union's candidate in the 2009 election. Was she not? Normally the media report in detail months in advance about every candidate for Chancellor. So I googled 'Chancellor' and 'Angela Merkel', and found nothing, not a single report on the choice of Merkel either at a party conference, or on account of a decision by the Union, or for any other reason. I now really wanted to know what was going on, so on 16 June 2009 I phoned the CDU's press office in Berlin to ask why there was nothing in the press about the Union's choice of a candidate. 'That's because no-one has been chosen yet', they said, but it was assumed that the present Chancellor would continue in the post. When I then asked about Roland Koch I was put through to another extension.

'There's nothing official yet', confirmed the CDU's deputy press spokeswoman Ina Diepold, 'but actually it's taken for granted that she will continue'. There wasn't going to be an official selection process; there was no need since Frau Merkel was and would remain the *de facto* candidate.

This made me wonder. It all seemed rather vague. And I somehow sensed an element of wariness in the reply. What normally happens is this: 'In the German Federal Republic the larger parties nominate their candidate for Chancellor prior to parliamentary elections. A party thus confirms that if the election result is positive for them their parliamentary party will elect that candidate for Chancellor.' (Wikipedia) Quite so. And yet what had been said to me seemed to suggest that the CDU did not want to say that this was so and that Frau Merkel had not been explicitly chosen by the Union to be their candidate for Chancellor, but rather only implicitly, if at all.

This was quite different in the case of the SPD's candidate, Frank-Walter Steinmeier. He was chosen as their candidate on 18 October 2008 during a party conference, thus signalling to the people: if you make the SPD the strongest party, then you will have Steinmeier as your Chancellor. This then counts as a promise. A search (on www.cdu.de) of CDU press releases for the whole previous year up to 16 June 2008 did not yield a single hit for 'candidate for Chancellor'. A similar search of the SPD yielded 180 hits. So for the 2009 parliamentary election the Union did indeed not have an official candidate for Chancellor! The statement from the CDU's press office meant that although Frau Merkel would 'compete' for election she had not been officially selected as the candidate. So there was also no promise that she would be Chancellor if the Union won. This could be interpreted as meaning that Merkel's popularity was being used to achieve success in the elections but that she would not necessarily be made Chancellor. Thus the door would at least be kept open for Bilderberger Roland Koch. Since this really did seem to be a preposterous operation I once again e-mailed the press spokesman of the CDU, Matthias Barner, on 16 June 2009:

> *Dear Herr Barner,*
>
> *May I please ask the following question re. the 2009 Federal Elections:*
> *Who is the Union's official candidate for Chancellor?*
>
> *Many thanks,*
> *Gerhard Wisnewski*

Reply: 'We shall be entering into the election contest under the leadership of our party chair and Federal Chancellor.' That's just it: 'entering into the election contest' is not synonymous with candidature for the Chancellorship. After all, a party enters into an election contest with all sorts of people, for example those who are ministers in the current government. So I sent off a further brief question: 'For the sake of complete clarity, should I take your reply to mean that the Federal Chancellor is therefore the official candidate for the chancellorship?' Such a simple question! It would take Herr Barner two seconds at most to tap 'Yes' into his computer, and be done with this irritating enquirer. But I was still waiting for that 'Yes' two days later. And I'm still waiting. Evidently the CDU/CSU union did not have a candidate for the chancellorship during the 2009 Federal Government election. And thus the door was still being held open for Bilderberger Roland Koch. What is also interesting is that against this background Koch was the federal deputy leader of the CDU, in other words Number Two in the terminology of German politics.

# Roland Koch *ante portas*

By the way, I sent my questionnaire twice each to Angela Merkel and Roland Koch (whether, when and why had they attended Bilderberg events, what goes on there, and so on). But with no result. I heard neither from the current Federal Chancellor nor from the current Minister-President of Hesse. At least not by post or e-mail. Instead an answer came, via a detour, from *Welt Online* of 4 October 2009. This stated: 'Chancellor Angela Merkel (CDU) hopes that Hesse's Minister-President Roland Koch will be Finance Minister. In her coalition discussions with the FDP she wants to ensure that in future it will be the CDU which manages that department, we are informed by the leadership of the Union.' In a single blinding flash this announcement made me aware of the whole ghoulish might of the Bilderbergers. I had been observing the process since their conference in Athens, and as time went on I had begun to think it unlikely that the Bilderbergers would set up ministers and chancellors directly. Roland Koch appeared to be rooted in Wiesbaden, the capital of the land of Hesse. Prior to the 2009 parliamentary elections he had declared that he definitely wished to remain in Hesse. Except that there was that door being kept secretly ajar in Berlin: the fact that Angela Merkel was not running for the chancellorship. For whom was the door being kept ajar? For Koch? Maybe. And this is no less likely considering that Koch was being pointed not in the direction of the chancellorship but towards the position of Finance Minister. After the way in which the 2009 federal elections had been so centred on Merkel, a direct transition to Koch as Chancellor would have been too abrupt. But perhaps he was to be gently introduced to the Federal Government prior to Angela Merkel's departure for, perhaps, the EU. On 3 October the Irish had after all agreed to the EU Reform Treaty, thus opening up the path towards a 'European Soviet Union'. Surely one post or another could be found there for Angela Merkel, just as had previously been successfully arranged in the case of the fired CSU party boss Edmund Stoiber.

But Koch's denial followed immediately: 'Very early on I said that my place lies in Wiesbaden', the media quoted him on 5 October. 'Asked whether he would refuse an offer from the Chancellor to join her new cabinet, Koch declared: "I have stated my position clearly",' reported *RP Online* on 5 October 2009. Actually, during the coalition discussions in Berlin between the Union and FDP, Koch put on a strong-man act. Here the deputy federal leader turned into Number One: 'The Minister-President of Hesse, Roland Koch, openly opposed Chancellor and party boss Angela Merkel during the party executive committee meeting and called for stringent economizing by the new Federal Government', reported *Financial Times Deutschland*, on 12 October 2009: 'Germany had been living beyond its means for decades, he said, thus indirectly criticising the financial policies of the Grand Coalition under Merkel's leadership.'

So the bogeyman from Wiesbaden was for the moment only casting his long shadow towards Berlin. The putsch against Angela Merkel failed in the end, and Roland Koch did not enter through the door being kept ajar in Berlin. Yet in his case, too, the fact remains that attendance at Bilderberg Conferences can often lead to significant career changes. After the failure of his rebellion he committed 'political suicide', resigning in 2010 from all his political posts and functions. And in 2011 he became Chairman of the Board of the German construction conglomerate Bilfinger Berger (turnover 8.5 milliard euros). One way of interpreting this might be to say that, for his total capitulation to Angela Merkel, he was rewarded with the Chair of Bilfinger Berger.

# 'One can't not communicate'

But now let's return to my questionnaire project. The three former Federal Chancellors Kohl, Schmidt and Schröder also replied, although these were not really replies since they merely declined. Schmidt's office wrote to say that he was 'too busy' to answer my questions about the Bilderberg Conferences. The same applied to retired Federal Chancellor Helmut Kohl: 'The Chancellor receives many similar requests from people researching his recollections. It is impossible for him to reply adequately to these requests, so I hope you will understand that he will be unable to comply with your wishes', wrote Kohl's office manager. Still, their participation at the Bilderberg Conferences was not denied, which would surely have been the case had they definitely not attended.

Gerhard Schröder's office even offered a confirmation: 'In his function as Federal Chancellor, Herr Schröder attended the Bilderberg Conference at Rottach-Egern on 6 May 2005. He gave a speech there, and departed immediately afterwards. He has not participated in any further conferences.' At last some clear information. But then Schröder's office fended off any likely 'conspiracy theories' that might have been framed by the perception of his visit to the Bilderbergers being linked in some way with his decision to call new elections soon afterwards: 'As you are surely aware, and as is also clearly explained in Herr Schröder's book *Entscheidungen* (Decisions), the decision to call for a new Federal election was taken immediately after the local elections in North-Rhine Westphalia on 22 May 2005.' Quite so. But on the other hand, politicians do not normally take a situation like that as a reason for putting their own power in question; they just go on ruling in the normal way. Of course red-green also had a majority in the Federal Government after the local elections in Lower Saxony. So why schedule new elections when one's party is obviously on a downward path? Would it not have been better to wait for the regular elections set for 2006 in order to gain ground once more? And why was that new election also forced by means of questionable constitutional stratagems? Surely the dissolution of the Federal Government and arrangement of new elections can only be set in train by a so-called 'false vote of confidence' in which parliament deprives a chancellor of confidence even though he still has a majority. In such a situation majority delegates 'purposely' vote against the Federal Chancellor or else abstain from voting. But when this takes place at the behest of the Federal Chancellor it is the best proof that the Chancellor is in fact recognized by the government's parliamentary groups as the leading figure. The 'false vote of confidence' thus makes a mockery of itself and is actually a proof of confidence in the Federal Chancellor whose path to new elections is approved by the Government's parliamentary groups. So there was no question of a loss of confidence. In reality the Chancellor's majority continued to exist as before in the Federal Government. In fact this is a special proof of confidence because at the behest of the Federal Chancellor the Government's parliamentary groups voluntarily relinquish their power and place themselves in the danger posed by new elections.

So we may well ask why, after the loss of the election in Lower Saxony, Schröder forced new Federal elections with the help of a dicey performance, thus putting the 'Chancellor's Throne' up for grabs without any real constitutional necessity. And we may equally well ask whether this had anything to do with the fact that he and the chancellorship candidate-in-waiting had, only three weeks previously and quite by coincidence, been guests at the same conference of strategic globalists, namely the Bilderberg Conference, and hence whether the lost elections in Lower Saxony were merely a pretext for introducing a change of power which was anyway already planned. The fact is that at the new elections in 2005 the SPD had, not unexpectedly, sustained considerable losses in comparison with the Federal elections of 2002. The scheduling of

Federal elections in the midst of a political crisis of the Chancellor's party can most certainly be viewed as a disguised resignation and a purposely set-in-train change of power. And so in the autumn of 2005 Schröder had to hand over the chancellorship to his 'Bilderberg lady-friend' Angela Merkel.

I also received a reply from Dieter Kastrup, guest of the Bilderbergers in 1991. From 1990 to 1995 he had been Secretary of State at the Foreign Office, from 1998 to 2001 Permanent Representative at the United Nations in New York, and since 11 April 2008 a member of the board of UNICEF-Germany. At least he was able to recall having attended a Bilderberg Conference 'but I absolutely do not remember when, where or on what subject'. He was sure he had travelled on official business, so his expenses would have been refunded by the taxpayer. 'No contacts of any duration were made. And there is no question of the participation having furthered my career', he wrote.

The next reply came from Professor Dr Volker Perthes, director of the foundation 'Wissenschaft und Politik' (Science and Politics). 'I have actually attended two Bilderberg Conferences as a consultant. Not being a regular participant I cannot comment in respect of most of your questions', he wrote. And: 'Even if I could, I would not necessarily feel motivated to do so in answer to a questionnaire such as yours.'

Evidently I still have a lot to learn with regard to motivating the Bilderbergers. And I was truly contrite after reading the next reply, which was from Theo Sommer, the grand old man of *Die Zeit*. 'I do not have sufficient time for a reply to your 27 questions. If I had, I might as well write a book about the Bilderbergers myself. However, I am busy with other projects just now.' And: 'Furthermore, most of your questions seem to me to be either insignificant or beside the point.' So there we have it: I'm quite simply incapable of asking Bilderbergers the right questions! And Sommer also wrote that he did not want to 'add any more fuel to further conspiracy theories'. How interesting! In other words, what he would be able to say might indeed fuel further conspiracy theories.

My own personal frontrunner among the letters of rejection came from Josef Joffe. In my opinion, this publisher-editor of *Die Zeit* is a member of too many foreign lobbying organizations; of so many, indeed, that one has to ask where his loyalties really lie. Joffe is a member of the management committee of the Leo Baeck Institute in New York and of the Ben-Gurion University of the Negev. He is also publisher-editor of the journal *The American Interest*. He is also involved with the American Council on Germany and with the American Institute for Contemporary German Studies.[38]

His reply to my questionnaire gave me the impression that I was getting on his nerves: 'Dear Herr Wisnewski, I cannot believe that anyone who really knows the Bilderbergers has replied to your questions. Bilderberg [Conferences] are confidential; otherwise people would not feel free to express their opinions candidly', he wrote, sounding irritated; and then concluded rudely: 'Further letters will not be answered.'

Well, no answer is also an answer. Or, as Paul Watzlawick put it: 'One can't not communicate'. By this means Joffe had certainly communicated volumes.

Actually, this applies in a greater or lesser degree to all the Bilderberg answers, none more so than the one from Rudolf Scharping, the unfortunate former head of the Social Democratic Party and unsuccessful 1994 candidate for the Chancellorship. Among the most inept replies from the Bilderbergers, his easily outshone that of Joffe. In 1999, when he attended the Bilderberg Conference, Scharping was Federal Defence Minister (from 1998 to 2002). Today he is not only President of the League of Cyclists but also business manager of Rudolf Scharping Strategy Consultants Ltd (RSBK GmbH) in Frankfurt-am-Main. Among others he advises Cerberus Capital Management (according to faz-finance.net of 12.5.2007) with which another Bilderberger and former Federal Defence Minister is also involved, namely Volker

Rühe of the Christian Democratic Union (CDU) (according to *manager magazin* of 15.10.2007). It appears, however, that Scharping's advice regarding communication does not extend to his own colleagues:

> *Dear Herr Wisnewski,* [wrote his office manager rudely] *you impute the attendance of Herr Scharping at 'Bilderberg Conferences'. Why? And on what legitimacy is your interest founded?*

Oops! Why so nervous? The more brusque the woman's tone became, the friendlier was mine, so I replied:

> *Dear Frau V.,*
>
> *Thank you so much for your reply. I have no intention of imputing anything. The fact is that Herr Scharping's name is included on a list of conference participants and I simply wanted to check whether he had actually participated in such a conference. So please do let me know if he did not, in fact, participate.*
>
> *If I may also ask, I would be interested to hear why Herr Scharping considers that my interest must be legitimated in some way.*
>
> *Apart from that I would greatly appreciate his kind reply to my questions.*
>
> *Meanwhile etc,*
> *With kind regards,*
> *Gerhard Wisnewski*

> *Dear Herr Wisnewski,* [she replied] *the only list you could have seen with Herr Scharping's name on it must have been an invitation list – and you cannot draw any further conclusions from that. Your further questions are therefore superfluous.*
>
> *With kind regards,*
> *V.*
> *Office Manager*

Normally I myself decide when further questions are superfluous. So I wrote back:

> *Dear Frau V.,*
>
> *Very many thanks for your reply. If I hear nothing further from you I shall assume that you deny any attendance by Herr Scharping at a Bilderberg Conference.*
>
> *With best wishes,*
> *Gerhard Wisnewski*

But a denial was evidently also not on the cards since otherwise the lady would not have written again. Instead, she now adopted a tactic of retaliation:

> *Dear Herr Wisnewski,*
>
> *We are always happy to reply to concrete enquiries.*
> *    You have unfortunately not answered the question as to the legitimacy of your questions, the reference being to professional information: journalist, literary agent, writer, TV author.*
>
> *With kind regards,*
> *V.*
> *Office Manager*

So presumably I had still not replied regarding the 'legitimacy' of my questions although the answer was obvious in my letter-head. The question remains as to why one must have a legitimate reason for asking Herr Scharping a few questions. So I wrote back:

> *Dear Frau V.,*
>
> *Thank you so much for taking the trouble to write and for your replies.*
> *    If your question regarding 'legitimacy' calls for further information about me, do please refer to the internet where you will find*

*plenty of references. I recommend the Google search-engine. Just enter the name 'Gerhard Wisnewski' and click on 'search'.*

*Apart from this, I am not aware that anyone requires specific 'legitimization' in order to ask a person a simple question, especially if that person has held public offices in the Federal Republic of Germany.*

*If citizens or journalists in the Federal Republic do require legitimization in order to ask Herr Scharping a question, or even several questions, I would be most grateful to learn about this and beg you to explain why such legitimization is required and what form it should take.*

*Your most recent e-mail has provided a sufficient answer in respect of my question concerning the need for a denial.*

*With many thanks and kind regards to Herr Scharping.*

*Gerhard Wisnewski.*

The lady had, after all, not denied Sharping's participation in the conferences. But as for the matter of communication, I would certainly not seek the advice of that office in this respect; the game of hide-and-seek launched by them would of course set every warning light flashing for a journalist. What on earth can have taken place at that Bilderberg Conference that made Rudolf Scharping's office manager go through all those contortions solely in order not to have to confirm the presence of her boss at that gathering?

The nervous replies of Scharping and Joffe comprise a considerable exception among the letters received from the Bilderbergers. Although most of the others barely provided concrete answers to any of the questions, they were all quite friendly. All the letters, though, were extremely cautiously formulated. Every new 'harmless' reply added to my impression that something utterly sinister must lie hidden behind them.

# The case of Rühe and Scharping

Since no minutes of the respective meetings are available one has to examine what circumstances individuals attending a meeting are involved in at the time of their Bilderberg attendance. The reason why Rudolf Scharping, for example, might not like remembering the Bilderberg Conference of 3 to 6 June 1999 at Sintra, Portugal, could be that those were the final days of the war in Kosovo which broke international law. Let's take things in sequence: Since minutes of the meetings are not available and since participants do not communicate anything (I never did receive any answers from Herr Rühe) one has to pay close attention to whatever Bilderbergers are involved in at about the time of their attendance.

In the 1990s, as soon as the Berlin Wall had fallen, Germany's role on the international stage was completely transformed. As quickly as possible the country abandoned its military reservations and began to participate in NATO involvements abroad, something which would have been unthinkable prior to the fall of the Wall. After World War II the doctrine of absolute abstinence from military involvement abroad held sway in the Federal Republic, with the Federal Armed Forces being seen as exclusively defensive. After all, the world did have rather bad memories of 'foreign involvements' by German armies. But now, within a few years, two Ministers of Defence were preparing the Germans and their armed forces for a new role as an international invasion force: Bilderbergers Volker Rühe (CDU) and Rudolf Scharping (SPD). Although they were members of parties purportedly opposed to one another, both those Ministers pursued the same militant NATO policies of the global elites.

The population were made familiar with foreign involvement by the military in two stages. First came missions displaying purely humanitarian aims under Volker Rühe. The second stage then finally exhibited the 'highest level of escalation', namely participation of the Federal German Armed Forces in an illegal and criminal war in Kosovo.

Unlike his predecessors Rupert Scholz and Gerhard Stoltenberg (both CDU), under whom strict abstinence from foreign involvement by the Federal forces was still the rule, Volker Rühe (CDU) was a regular attendee at Bilderberg Conferences for almost the whole duration of his period of office from 1992 to 1998. It was he who had the task of accustoming the Germans to the word and the idea of 'foreign military involvement' or, more accurately: involvement outside NATO's area of involvement. He succeeded in this virtually without any opposition because exclusively 'humanitarian missions' were chosen. The Minister of Defence regularly played 'the philanthropist', for example posing for photos in front of Transall's military transport aircraft from which aid was in process of being unloaded somewhere in the world. For example:

– April 1992: Deployment of 140 medical personnel to Phnom Penh to care for members of the United Nations Transitional Authority in Cambodia (UNTAC),
– from 1993: Participation in a UN peace mission to Somalia,
– 1994: Participation in an airlift of supplies for Rwandan refugees.

Supplies for refugees: who would want to object to that? No-one, of course. So the Minister gave one frank interview after another in war-torn regions in keeping with the motto: What do you expect? Should we not have given aid? Thus in only a few years the subject of 'out of area deployment of the Federal military' was duly kicked into the long grass both journalistically and psychologically.

Despite the 1998 change of government and the entry into office of a 'red-green' coalition under Gerhard Schröder (SPD), there was, interestingly, no change in these policies. Quite to the contrary, in fact. A common thread runs from Rühe's (CDU) 'humanitarian' foreign interventions right through to the not so humanitarian 'military interventions' of Scharping (SPD). Indeed, Volker Rühe's 'humanitarian interventions' were simply the reverse side of one and the same coin. The machinations of the SPD's Defence Minister Scharping were dependent upon those of his predecessor Rühe. Which only goes to prove yet again that whatever the Federal Government in power might do is irrelevant; what counts is above all the strategic agenda of the globalists.

As already mentioned, Rudolf Scharping was a guest at the 1999 Bilderberg Conference from 3 to 6 June. As the lists are not necessarily complete we may assume that he perhaps also attended earlier meetings. As described, his office did not wish to commit itself. The fact is that Bilderberger and globalist Scharping played an important part in selling the spring 1999 war in Kosovo to Germany and the world. As a part of this war NATO forces attacked Yugoslavia without a mandate from the United Nations. Justification for this intervention were putative serious human rights violations by Yugoslavia in its fight against the terrorists of the Kosovo Liberation Army (UÇK) in the province of Kosovo.

This war was contrived by those situated at the upper end of the global chain of command, the puppet-masters of the Project for a New American Century (PNAC), which in turn has links with the Bilderbergers. Just as in the matter of Iraq, these people wrote an urgent letter to US President Bill Clinton on 20 September 1998, as ever 'out of deep concern' regarding the human rights of, on this occasion, the Albanian population of Kosovo. The Serbs had driven them from their homes and farmsteads and they would be likely to starve during the approaching winter. Why the West could just stand by and watch this happening was inexplicable. As later in the case of Saddam Hussein, the PNAC had already in 1998 recognized Yugoslav President Slobodan Milosevic as a villain who ought to be removed: 'There can be no peace and stability in the Balkans so long as Slobodan Milosevic remains in power', wrote the PNAC strategists who, of course, wanted only one thing, democracy, democracy and yet again democracy. 'We believe that the time has come for the United States to distance itself from Milosevic and actively support in every way possible his replacement by a democratic government committed to ending ethnic violence.' We know what happened next: Beginning in the spring of 1999 NATO bombed Yugoslavia and, just like Saddam Hussein, Milosevic ended up as a corpse – in his case in the prison of the War Crimes Tribunal in The Hague, where he had arrived exactly in accordance with PNAC's scenario ('The U.S. should vigorously support The Hague Tribunal's investigation of Milosevic as war criminal') and where he died in 2006 in unexplained circumstances.

Federal Defence Minister Rudolf Scharping functioned as the top 'salesman' of this PNAC war. According to an ARD documentary ('It started with a lie'), it is alleged that Bilderberger Scharping supplied the public with false information about what the Yugoslavs were doing in Kosovo. He said that prior to NATO's intervention there had been a 'humanitarian catastrophe' in Kosovo with 250,000 refugees within Kosovo and 'far more than 400,000 refugees overall and an as yet unknown number of dead'. Heinz Loquai, German General and observer of the OSCE (Organization for Security and Co-operation in Europe), is documented as saying the opposite, namely that 'a humanitarian catastrophe that justified being categorized as a human rights violation was not happening in Kosovo prior to the onset of the war'.

Researches by the TV film makers also concluded that other infringements and massacres of Kosovans by Serbs claimed by Scharping to have taken place did not happen:

– 'The fiction of the Serbian concentration camp': According to Scharping the Serbs had set up a concentration camp in a football stadium in Pristina, capital city of Kosovo, where they 'shot schoolteachers in front of their pupils'. The film makers visited Shaban Kelmendi who had a direct view into the stadium from his balcony. 'There was not a single prisoner or hostage', said

Kelmendi. 'The stadium was always only a landing place for helicopters.'

— 'The fiction of the Rugovo massacre': According to Scharping, the Serbian 'Special Police' had massacred civilians in the rural village of Rugovo. Yet according to a secret situation report by his own ministry there had been a 'fight' there, say the documentary film makers. The OSÇE observer already mentioned also said in the film: 'It was obvious that this was not a massacre of civilians; UÇK commanders themselves had said that fighters for the great Albanian cause had died there. It was the German Defence Minister who interpreted this as having been a massacre.'

— 'The fiction of "Operation Horseshoe"': According to Scharping, Serbian troops deployed in the form of a horseshoe kettled Albanian civilians and expelled them from Kosovo. However, the documentation quoted the OSÇE observer Heinz Loquai, already mentioned, as saying that even according to experts at the Defence Ministry a horseshoe plan had never existed.

Jochen Scholz, a lieutenant colonel at the Defence Ministry in 1999, who 'worked very closely with those who were observing the situation in the Balkans', had, before the war began, also

> stated that the actual situation in Kosovo had not tallied with what the politicians had announced. We are all familiar with the terminology current at the time, also in public debates: ethnic cleansing, genocide, expulsion. These are the catchphrases for a humanitarian catastrophe. In fact and in reality it is confirmed by all the situation plans current in the Ministry, with which the Minister was of course familiar, that what was going on in Kosovo was a civil war, barbarous as such wars always are, but nevertheless a civil war in which all the ethnic groups were suffering equally and in which all the protagonists were equally involved — both the UÇK and the Serb forces …

The final sentence in the assessment of the situation by the Office for Military Intelligence on 22 March 1999, two days before the commencement of war, stated: 'There are still no signs of ethnic cleansing in Kosovo.' So much for the propaganda that justified the war.[39]

'Rudolf Scharping certainly did a good job', the documentation mentioned above quoted the NATO Spokesman at the time, Jamie Shea, as saying:

> The political leaders now played the decisive part as regards public opinion. They are the democratically elected representatives. They knew what information was important for public opinion in their country.

# Sorcerer and sorcerer's apprentice

So much for Bilderbergers Rühe and Scharping. But other Bilderbergers, too, have behaved in quite bizarre ways during the years of
their involvement with the conferences.

Let's take the former boss of Daimler, a subsidiary of Deutsche
Bank, Jürgen Schrempp. In 1998 he fused his company with the
limping American Chrysler enterprise, thus becoming boss of
DaimlerChrysler AG while giving away or losing untold sums.
(Interestingly, the outrageous spelling of the combined names is
enough to show that nothing seems to fit together.) According to my
records, Schrempp attended Bilderberg Conferences annually from
1994 to 2007 with two exceptions, mutating from Chairman of the
Board of Daimler-Benz AG to (from 1998) Chairman of the Board of
DaimlerChrysler AG. His attendance at Bilderberg Conferences
ended in 2007, the year in which Daimler sold Chrysler again, to an
investment company called Cerberus or 'Hound of Hell'. That
'Hound of Hell', too, was a guest at Bilderberg Conferences, for
example in the guise of former German Defence Minister Volker
Rühe.

Might Schrempp have been 'prompted' to sell Chrysler during his
attendance at the Bilderberg Conference? To this day it's still
inexplicable to me why he ever bought it. By 1979 Chrysler was
almost bust and could only be rescued by the US Congress. Of
course I also sent my questionnaire to Jürgen Schrempp. It was not
difficult to find his address since a healthy 65-year-old senior citizen
of that name beams out at us from his own website, juergen-
schrempp.com., where he vaunts his worthiness and decorations
from, among others, the Axel Springer Verlag (represented at the
Bilderbergers by, among others, Mathias Döpfner and Gerhard
Cromme), and the Burda Verlag (represented at the Bilderbergers

by Hubert Burda). There are also a good many globalist prizes from 'our American friends', such as the Vernon A. Walters Award from the German-American Network Atlantic Bridge.

Vernon A. Walters was something like a sacred cow of the secret service world. He was a member of the American Secret Service (from 1972 to 1976 deputy chief of the CIA) and a 'diplomat' (which often stands for the same thing). In his youth he had attended Stonyhurst Catholic boarding and day school in England, guided by the principles of the Society of Jesus, a top-class elite training centre which, over the course of its 400-year history, had produced or educated three saints, twelve beatified persons, 22 martyrs, seven archbishops, one Peruvian president, one prime minister of New Zealand, one signatory to the American Declaration of Independence, and a good many other politicians and even European monarchs. He spoke six Western European languages, which socialized him as a globalist, and later added Russian and basic Chinese.

According to reports, this devout Catholic attended Mass every day even, as far as possible, when travelling. This man with the brutal mastiff's face had never been married and, supposedly, never had a sexual relationship with either a woman or a man. Not even the French (!) secret service had succeeded in seducing him either with women or men; so they finally had to accept that Walters was not interested in such things. Is this truly something admirable? Or does a person like that vent sexual frustration elsewhere? The priest at his home church had described him as a 'chaste bachelor', we read in *Crisis Magazine* of February 2005, which adds that he knew only one passion – chocolate. Surely, indeed, the food of the frustrated!

This rather reminds us of Joseph Hieronim Retinger. Good old Vernon Walters, a Johnny on the spot in all imperialist and globalist matters, had evidently also sworn an oath of chastity. Which means that as well as attending a Jesuit boarding school he was himself a Jesuit! And he did what Jesuits always do, he trampled other nations underfoot. The notorious CIA boss under President Reagan, William Casey (student at Fordham University), was another 'CIA Jesuit'.

So with the Vernon A. Walters Award, Jürgen Schrempp had received an honest-to-goodness American secret-service-and-Jesuit prize. And he then also received the Global Leadership Award of the American Institute for Contemporary German Studies. Many American and German Bilderbergers bump into one another as members of that Institute's board of directors, among others Josef Joffe of *Die Zeit*, Klaus Kleinfeld (temporary chairman of the Siemens board), Wolfgang Ischinger (Munich Security Conference), and Lothar Späth. Schrempp accumulated all kinds of prizes from his Bilderberg mates, for example the Golden Steering Wheel Award of *Bild am Sonntag*, and the Millennium Bambi Prize of Burda Verlag. No wonder he beams out from his website like the famous Cheshire cat. He is evidently untroubled by having dropped the essentially German firm of Daimler into one of its greatest crises. And why should he be troubled? He appears to have extricated himself long ago from German connections and identities. Without perhaps being fully aware of what he was doing, was he chiefly hoping to found not so much a commercial enterprise as a Jesuit project by creating a 'world enterprise'? So rather than being commercial, were his motives perhaps rather more ideological? I was unfortunately unable to ask these questions because I never received an answer to my enquiries.

One does wonder what to think when the captain of Daimler, Germany's industrial battleship, keeps accumulating (as a counter manoeuvre?) 'globalist' prizes named partly after Jesuits (like Walters) or after those influenced by them. This is also true of the Woodrow Wilson Award. The former American President (1913 to 1921) was under the influence of a man named Edward Mandell House who is everywhere described as an 'undercover Jesuit'. Wilson himself said that House was his 'alter ego'. The designation 'undercover Jesuit' may have derived from the fact that although he was married and wealthy, his typical networking behaviour was very much that of a Jesuit. 'His diary records meals with Henry James, Edith Wharton and Rudyard Kipling, as well as with the virtuoso pianist Ignazy Jan Paderewski, who became President of Poland', we read in a biography by Godfrey Hodgson. 'He mingled with politicians, generals, bankers, academics, journalists, and society hostesses in New York, Paris and London.' This sounds almost as though House had founded an earlier form of Bilderberg club, for this exactly resembles the composition of the Bilderbergers after 1954 – with the exception, perhaps, of the 'society hostesses'. 'Though a sickly man and certainly not a flamboyant one, he had a flair for making friends who appreciated his discretion, respected his views, and valued his counsel', wrote economic scientist Robert Higgs. 'His talent for winning friends and influencing people would remain the basis of his remarkable achievements throughout his life. He was, in today's lingo, a very smooth operator, appreciated all the more because he clearly had no desire to displace the king he had just helped to place on the throne. The power he sought was the power behind the throne.'[40]

This might equally well be a description of Retinger. House was never President – but he made Presidents. He began by helping no fewer than four men to attain the post of Governor of Texas while guiding them behind the scenes. Then (1910–11) he selected the Governor of New Jersey, Woodrow Wilson, for a more ambitious project: the assault on the presidency. Not only did House play an important role as Wilson's electoral strategist. He also smoothed internal strife among the Democrats – another Jesuit speciality. Once President, Wilson gave House a considerably free hand in filling cabinet posts, not only choosing him as Secretary of State but also offering him any other cabinet position he might want. But House declined, 'electing to continue working in the shadows – as the President's preferred adviser.'[41]

So House soon came to be rated as the actual President of the United States. His (or rather Wilson's) period of office saw such signal developments as the founding of the Federal Reserve Bank in 1913 and the entry of the USA into World War I in 1917. House was also involved in other globalist projects such as the founding of the already-mentioned foreign policy lobby, the Council on Foreign Relations, which subsequently came to select not only the majority of US Presidents and higher CIA staff, but also many of the US attendees at Bilderberg Conferences.

# Mr Kopper's protégé

So much, then, for Schrempp's Woodrow Wilson Award. But Schrempp, loaded though he was with imperialist and Jesuit trumpery, was in no way an independent global player but rather one who received 'advice', initially from Hilmar Kopper, for many years spokesman of the Board of Deutsche Bank. On the basis of financial interrelationships, the reputedly so mighty Daimler company was regarded as the 'industrial branch' of Deutsche Bank which did, from time to time, have a say in matters concerning the car manufacturer: for example, who should be President of the Board. In 1995, top-Bilderberger Kopper helped to push through top-'failure' Jürgen Schrempp for that post. 'Kopper had done all he could in support of his strategy to transform the national car manufacturer into a player on the world stage', reported *Süddeutsche Zeitung* on 3 April 2007. And not only that. Bilderberger Kopper stuck by Schrempp 'even when the management had become aware that the road to America and the road to Japan were both wrong, so that open resistance to Schrempp was beginning to build'.

How strange: Appearing with hindsight as having been guided by remote control, Schrempp it is alleged, in this report,

> was granted almost complete free rein in running Daimler because Kopper let him get away with virtually anything. Despite his lack of success, Schrempp under Kopper was soon one of Germany's most highly paid managers. Kopper even overstretched the law on stock companies on behalf of his favourite. Quite a few people regarded as scandalous the way in which he once helped his friend to obtain a premature extension of his management contract. He had permitted

Schrempp to resign formally but then take up the reins again immediately under a new contract with a new term. This had led to concern in the business world because it is the job of a supervisory board to discipline a boss, not to admire him and reach agreements with him that artificially extend the term of his tenure. (süddeutsche.de 3.4.2007)

It really beggars belief: The boss of the mighty Deutsche Bank holds a protective hand over a sorcerer's apprentice who is evidently trying to turn too ambitious a cartwheel.

'Insiders claim', continued *Süddeutsche Zeitung*, 'that Kopper was so enthusiastic about shirt-sleeved Schrempp because of the similarity between them. Schrempp had begun his professional career with Daimler as a car mechanic but he was also the type of manager who dared take decisions that were out of the ordinary.'

Well, that's one way of looking at it. While Schrempp toddled off year after year to the Bilderberg Conferences, his great mentor Kopper was already there as a member of the so-called Executive Committee. Good old Herr Kopper, mentor of globalist sorcerer's apprentice Schrempp, was a very big shot among the Bilderbergers where global players from both sides of the Atlantic said good-day and also good-night to one another. Actually, it was night which soon descended upon the megalomaniacal plans of the one-time car-mechanic. Daimler withdrew in disgrace from its various interests, and Schrempp's 'world concern' soon proved itself a dreadful flop, at least when regarded as an enterprising concept. It was, though, perhaps less of a flop when seen as the ideological concept of global strategists. Here it was not a matter of money but of the equally ancient and meanwhile frequently publicized 'One World Ideology', or, one might as well say: *the* 'One World Ideology' of the Jesuits.

Of course I also wanted to hear from both Schrempp and Kopper about the role played by the Bilderbergers in their 'enterprising' decisions. Nothing was heard from Schrempp in his comfortable retirement, but Kopper did at least confirm that he was on the Executive Committee of the Bilderbergers and that he had even been their Treasurer. For the rest, he begged me to understand that he 'wished to adhere to the time-tested Bilderberg rule of with-holding information about the participants as well as the content of the conferences'. Once again I was full of understanding. But he for his part should be sympathetic if I have totally *mis*-understood the background described above as being an expression of some kind of wheeling and dealing and an evidently hugely detrimental power network.

But let us not forget that this is merely one diminutive solar system in the Bilderberg cosmos. Another such was that of former CEO of Deutsche Post Klaus Zumwinkel.

# Klaus Zumwinkel – another sorcerer's apprentice

Among the Bilderbergers we frequently discover German bosses who suddenly feel called to (even) higher things, and then make a real dog's dinner of millions and billions invested in world-enterprises. This also appears to be the case of Klaus Zumwinkel, former boss of Deutsche Post AG, the German post office. Like Schrempp, Zumwinkel changed during his time as a Bilderberger (according to my records between 2002 and 2007). In the year of his first Bilderberg attendance, the German Language Association 'honoured' him with the title of 'Chief Adulterator of the German Language' for his introduction of anglicisms such as 'Global Mail', 'Stampit' or 'Freeway'. From 2003 onwards, Deutsche Post AG was permitted to share in the profits of the Iraq war through the daily transport of 30 to 50 tonnes of forces' mail to Iraq for the US military. It is highly unusual for such a military task to be carried out by a foreign enterprise. During the same year the boss of Deutsche Post AG became the boss of Deutsche Post World Net AG. And Klaus Zumwinkel was awarded the 2003 Industry Leadership Award for the successful development of Deutsche Post from a loss-making national agency into a global logistics enterprise. So our friend Klaus, too, was suddenly beginning to dream of a world enterprise. In 2002, Zumwinkel's first year with the Bilderbergers, Deutsche Post AG developed its share of the American logistics firm DHL to the extent of finally taking it over entirely. At around the same time CEO Zumwinkel also declared that Deutsche Post was planning a large increase in its business with Asia. (KEP-nachrichten, 24.5.2002)

But 'initial losses' soon began to occur: 'The initial losses from Deutsche Post's engagement with the American market were much higher than expected, and this is having a knock-on effect for all branches of business', wrote *Spiegel Online* on 7 November 2004. 'Instead of an increase in business of at least 20 per cent, Deutsche Post now estimates a maximum decrease of this magnitude for the current year. At the end of September 2004 Deutsche Post announced estimated losses of 500 million euros; 300 million had been the estimate. In the third quarter, according to the Thursday report, profits in the express division tumbled by almost 68 per cent to a meagre nine million euros.'

'Sorcerer's apprentice Zumwinkel' was honoured by the globalists, of course. On 29 November 2004, in New York, he received the 2004 John J. McCloy Award of the American Council on Germany 'in recognition of the increasing presence of Deutsche Post World Net in the USA and for his extraordinary contribution to the intensification of German-American commercial relations.' (*DHL Presse,* 28.11.2004) This was no exaggeration. As a step towards becoming a global player Zumwinkel had used all the billions in profit made by the steady and reliable German postal business. Unlike Zumwinkel, John J. McCloy was a genuine global player. Having initially been President of the World Bank, McCloy had become High Commissioner for Germany in 1949 and proceeded to amnesty condemned Nazi war criminals such as Alfried Krupp von Bohlen und Halbach, Friedrich Flick and Ernst von Weizsäcker. Later on he became boss of Bilderberg co-founder David Rockefeller's Chase Manhattan Bank. And for 16 years (until 1970) McCloy was boss of the mighty Council on Foreign Relations (CFR), a position in which Rockefeller subsequently succeeded him. As a member of the so-called Warren Commission, McCloy was also involved in the cover-up relating to the assassination of Kennedy (1963). Having initially been sceptical regarding the theory of a lone perpetrator, he allowed himself to be 'convinced' by, of all men, Allen Dulles, member of the CFR and founder of the CIA.

The Zumwinkel Prize was endowed by the American Council on Germany (ACG), which included – by coincidence, if you like – on its board a good number of Bilderbergers such as, for example, top Bilderberger Henry Kissinger, as well as Paul A. Volcker and Richard Holbrooke among others. The Young Leaders Programme of the ACG also, by the way, produced the new German Defence Minister Karl-Theodor zu Guttenberg. So the location of his true bosses ought to be obvious. Bilderbergers Wolfgang Ischinger (1978), Matthias Wissmann (1982) and the fanatical 'Atlanticist' Friedbert Pflüger (1982) are also former 'Young Leaders' of the ACG.

One was mutually acquainted and one quite naturally belonged to the same extended family which unfortunately had little to do with one's home country and its interests. So it did not really matter that, four years after Zumwinkel had received the globalists' award, the 'initial losses' of US involvement in Deutsche Post had mutated into a disaster of millions; after all, the money had not disappeared, it had simply gone elsewhere:

> A few years ago Klaus Zumwinkel had been arrogantly boasting that he would entice the customers away from the USA's leading competitors FedEx and UPS [wrote the website of *Der Stern* on 25 January 2008]. But under pressure from his capital financiers the boss of Deutsche Post is now forced to admit to having made a miscalculation ... *Financial Times Deutschland* (FTD) is now quantifying the amount of the accumulated deficit since 2003 as being up to 7 milliard euros. And now the financial markets have been taken by surprise this week with the news of a special amortisation in the US express business for the year 2007 of 600 million euros. (stern.de 25.1.2008)

'However, a radical cut-off of the USA in a total withdrawal, as had been demonstrated by Daimler's rejection of Chrysler, was unlikely', wrote the *Stern* website. Well, if we replace 'unlikely' by 'unavoidable' we shall be closer to the truth. Hardly a year later all that remained of the dream of world enterprise was an 'American nightmare'. (*Welt Online*, 11.11.2008) The new boss of Deutsche

Post, Frank Appel, had 'cancelled all the plans of his meanwhile fired predecessor Klaus Zumwinkel and closed down the American adventure. Many thousands of employees of the daughter enterprise DHL are losing their jobs in the USA. The reputation of the express service which was to have given its rivals United Parcel Service and FedEx the shivers in North America is finally ruined'.

As in the case of Dieter Zetsche with Daimler, Frank Appel now had to check the finances of Deutsche Post and sweep up the debris. 'In the end this chapter in the history of the enterprise will have cost about eight milliard euros, the equivalent of four years of profit by the letter-post business of the enterprise', *Welt Online* tells us.

Via his lawyer Hanns Feigen, I also sent Klaus Zumwinkel my small questionnaire concerning the meaning, purpose and influence of the Bilderbergers on his career and his business decisions. But somehow it does not appear to have reached him in his Italian exile, for the former Global Player has so far not responded.

# The 'Global Enterprise'

If it is true that only innocuous conversations 'about general mat-ters' take place at Bilderberg summits, then the question still remains as to why these conversations have to be kept so strictly secret. The truth of the matter is of course that these 'private exchanges of opinion' are not at all as innocuous as the Bilder-bergers would have us believe. We discover this when we do suc-ceed in casting a glance behind the scenes of the conferences when, for example, a participant more or less by accident lets slip a few remarks, or when someone smuggles conference papers out of the venue, or even records one of the lectures that then reappears in some book or other which scarcely anyone reads. A lecture of this kind is to be found in the fourth volume of a largely unknown book *Synarchy Movement of Empire* by Pierre Beaudry and published in 2005.

Here we learn that the enterprises DaimlerChrysler/Mitsubishi and Deutsche Post World Net were only the first tentative steps of the Bilderberg elites on the path towards an all-embracing World Enterprise. DaimlerChrysler/Mitsubishi would have combined large portions of the European, American and Asian car industry in a single enterprise. Permission by the European Commission for such a fusion would have been merely a matter of form since of course numerous former and current EU Commissioners are also Bilderbergers, and because it is known that the European Com-mission is not a democratically elected body which can be called to account by its citizens. First and foremost it appears that these enterprises were created more for ideological than for commercial reasons. This is demonstrated not only by the failure of these concepts but also by the incompatibility of the building blocks involved (e.g. Chrysler). Audacious houses of cards were constructed out of the enterprises involved; they reached right up to the stratosphere but soon collapsed in upon one another. Characteristically, Jürgen Schrempp used a religious concept and a religious idea in describing his combination of DaimlerChrysler AG as 'a marriage made in heaven'. His still unbroken pride in this may well have to do with having been involved in one of the most daring commercial experiments of his day – the construction of a commercial Tower of Babel. That tower only endured for a few years, from 1998 to 2007, before Schrempp's successor, Dieter Zetsche (incidentally not a Bilderberger), sorted out and sold off the fragments to the best of his ability. Nevertheless, with his Operation 'World Enterprise' Schrempp had written a chapter of commercial and enterprise history. To describe him as having failed is justified only from the point of view of shareholders and personnel, i.e. the 'ants' who, as a result of the operation, lost 50 milliards of euros (stock-exchange losses of DaimlerChrysler during Schrempps term of office according to *Spiegel Online* on 28.7.2005) and more than 14,000 places of work. But matters look very different from the point of view of the globalists. For them, Schrempp is a hero.

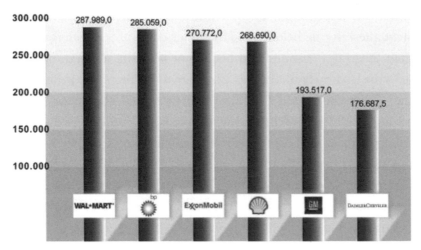

*World enterprises with Bilderberg connections: BP, Shell, DaimlerChrysler – three of the highest profit-making enterprises (profit in milliards of US dollars in 2005)*

From the point of view of the Bilderberg Conferences founded by the Jesuits, these enterprises were simply in advance of their time. As with the United States of America or with Europe, global unification must also take place at the commercial level of enterprises. It is obvious that by this means enterprises come into being which squash individual human beings like flies or like the ants mentioned above, be they shareholders, personnel or customers. Personnel, customers and shareholders are merely the potential from which the management of the enterprise draws its strength and which it leads – just as a general leads an army. By the very fact of being superhuman, such monster enterprises become inhuman. In the face of gigantic structures, be they political, as in the case of the EU, or commercial, as in the case of the World Enterprise, they diminish the individual human being to the dimension of an insect. This is perfectly simple arithmetic.

However, the idea of a World Enterprise did not arise in the brain of a Hilmar Kopper or even of a Jürgen Schrempp. It was presented thirty years earlier at a Bilderberg meeting – from 26 to 28 April 1968 at Mont Tremblant, Canada. There, according to Pierre Beaudry (*Synarchy Movement of Empire*), a certain George Ball spoke about the 'implications of the world enterprise'. Ball was no transient guest, for he belonged to the inner circle of the Bilderbergers, their Steering Committee. In his business life he was a director in both the leading banks of the day, Lehman Brothers and Kuhn Loeb Inc. 'In essence', said Beaudry, 'Ball presented an outline of the advantages of a new-colonial world economic order based on the concept of a "world company", and described some of the obstacles that needed to be eliminated for its success. According to Ball, the first and most important thing that had to be eliminated was "the archaic political structure of the nation state".'[42] In other words, essentially that with which the Jesuits had for ever been at loggerheads. But the national state poses no danger to world peace. On the contrary, it stands in the way of global economic and political power, i.e. of global dictatorship. The small structures of national states hinder the expansion of enterprises and of a central political and economic power.

'To be productive', said Ball according to Beaudry, 'we must begin our inquiry by explicitly recognizing the lack of phasing between development of the world company — a concept responding to modern needs — and the continued existence of an archaic political structure of nation states ...'

According to Beaudry, it had been clear to Ball that the structure of the nation state, together with the idea of public welfare, represented the chief hindrance to endeavours to plunder the earth and above all the poor and the world's most feeble states. In addition, the nation state is the chief hindrance along the path towards a neo-colonial 'world empire'.[43]

Essentially, Beaudry claimed, Bilderberger Ball was referring to the natural conflict between corporate interests and national welfare.

The priority of a world company, he was saying, evidently rested on unhindered international free trade, in other words on the British standard of buy cheap and sell dear. In Ball's view, national governments had been the problem; their priorities differed from those of the exploitation practised by corporations. A corporation's so-called 'host countries' exercised unfair opposition to them with their public welfare concerns.[44]

According to Beaudry, globalization is therefore merely 'a new name for a new colonial realm' which in this case encompasses the globe as a whole. When we hear this we are no longer surprised that so many members of royal houses are involved with the Bilderbergers or indeed why the conferences were actually founded by a royal personage. Whether they are Prince Philippe of Belgium, Queen Beatrix of the Netherlands, or Sofia, Queen of Spain, these monarchs comprise one of the most important groups among the Bilderbergers.

Ball's misconception with regard to a global economy, wrote Beaudry, was founded on the wish to invest corporations with rights which would enable them to plunder the world as far as possible without limitations imposed by governments. This was the central conflict between the world of business on the one hand and governments on the other. This was Ball's belief and his religion.[45]

Chief Bilderberger Ball could not stand local governments, for, as he said, 'the responsibility of a local government, on the other hand, is for the health and progress of the national economy to which the world company frequently contributes only a very small share; in addition, it is subject to emotions of national pride, to pressures from local interests claiming special advantages, and − if it is the government of a newly independent state − to an almost pathological fear of foreign economic dominance that might lead to what is mystically referred to as neo-colonialism.'[46]

'Obviously the world company creates quite different problems for the new, poor nations of the Southern Hemisphere than for the industrialized countries of the North', says Ball. 'Since a world company is more likely to be the dominant element of economic power in a small nation than a large one, the prosperity of many less-developed countries is left heavily dependent on decisions made by managements of world companies located five or six thousand miles away. When, as is often the case, an extractive industry is involved, the problem is given an additional emotional overlay by the fact that the world company disposes of what it traditionally regards as the national patrimony.'[47]

For Ball, says Beaudry, these are 'obviously' terrible problems that must be 'ironed out in order to give free reign to economic predators because they are often in conflict with national development plans of the host country'.[48]

Ball also dealt with Europe in his lecture. At a time when most people thought the concept of 'peaceful coexistence' referred to the coexistence of dangerous, heavily-armed power blocks, he was thinking rather of a peaceful coexistence of corporations and governments, as though these structures were profoundly at odds with one another. Although Europe had made great strides since its unification, Ball said: 'I doubt that European commerce will be able to establish itself if conditions are not created that enable Europe to become fertile soil for new world corporations.'[49]

And to this we may add world corporations à la Daimler-Chrysler. Thirty years later, in 1998, Europe had evidently reached the stage when it became possible to permit such monster enterprises to come into existence. 'Until Europe achieves greater political unity, I doubt, however, that European business will be able to make adequate progress toward a more ample structure', said Ball.[50]

'In other words', comments Beaudry, 'European nations have to abandon their national interest and must move as rapidly as possible toward political supranational institutions that will permit them to join Americans in the systematic looting of the continent, from within as well as from without.'[51]

Taking this to its logical conclusion leads us to assume that Bilderberger Ball did not think much of nations, including the American nation. Of course, because of its size and the gigantic shared market of 50 States, the latter does provide a better habitat for large corporations, although only until they attain a specific size. In other words, a global enterprise resembles a body-builder whose national shirt is stretched across his muscle-bound chest until it splits. Or, more critically still, such commercially muscle-bound hunks are capable of splitting any number of shirts, i.e. national states. So a global enterprise can become a weapon with which to attack a national state, outdoing it to such an extent by its international standing that it begins to appear obsolete and of questionable value.

People like Ministers Scharping and Rühe or corporation bosses such as Schrempp and Zumwinkel, who in some ways acted counter to the interests of their enterprises, their personnel and their shareholders, are not accidents among the Bilderbergers but are, actually, in rather good company. Other German members or guests have been:

— politicians Schily and Schäuble, who as Interior Ministers both participated in curtailing civil rights,

— media bosses Mathias Döpfner, Josef Joffe, Theo Sommer and Matthias Nass as well as Hubert Burda, who represent a large part of German and European media power,

— former extra-parliamentary activist and subsequently Federal Foreign Minister Joschka Fischer, who exchanged the 'Putztruppe' of his pre-parliamentary times for work with NATO,

— former Secretary of State in the Ministry of Defence and supporter of the Iraq war, the CDU's trans-Atlantic scandal blockhead Friedbert Pflüger, ardent fan of the European Union and one of the initiators of the convention for the elaboration of the European Constitution.

It would be hard to imagine any of these individuals acting in the interests of any nation, let alone their own. The interests they appear to support are those of global networks.

# Part 5

# THE GLOBAL GOVERNMENT

Are the Bilderbergers a 'clandestine global government'? Surely not: 'I am amused by the imputations and speculations that appear year after year in connection with the Bilderberg Conferences', says staunch 'Atlanticist' and Bilderberger Eckart von Klaeden, a CDU politician for foreign affairs and also a member of the wheeling-and-dealing American-German Atlantik-Brücke e.V. (Atlantic Bridge registered society). 'All such ideas are pure speculation', says the Burda Verlag's Bilderberg journal *Focus*. (*Focus Online*, no date) And there's no point in even trying to find out anything about the secret conferences on the websites of Bilderberg media *Bild-Zeitung*, *Die Zeit*, or *Die Welt*.

# TC — The expansion of the Bilderbergers

In fact the Bilderbergers had their eye on the whole world from the very beginning and were planning to set up further global brain-trusts. A report on the third conference, at Garmisch-Partenkirchen in 1955 records: 'It was felt that there must grow up not only a better understanding between the countries of the Western Alliance but a closer contact and better understanding with the Asian and African countries... There was a strong current of opinion also that there might be great value in arranging a subsequent meeting between the leaders of mind and spirit of the East and West in an atmosphere similar to that of the Bilderberg series of conferences.'[52]

This indicates that the Asian and African regions were to be included in the Bilderberg process, and this did indeed come about, in 1973. In that year, the key man of the Bilderbergers, David Rockefeller, founded the so-called Trilateral Commission (TC). If the Council on Foreign Relations is the father of the Bilderbergers, then the Trilateral Commission is, as it were, their child. The 'bilateral' Bilderberg personnel of Europe and the USA now met with a third group, the elites of the third-largest economic region in the world, Japan. Hence the name Trilateral Commission.

## A clandestine super-government?

It would be an error to speak of a super-government, wrote Bilderberger Theo Sommer in 1977, in a long-forgotten article in *Die Zeit*, on the occasion of the fifth anniversary of the founding of the Trilateral Commission: 'What is true, however, is that a useful plateau for encounter and exchange has come into being over and above national and international bureaucracies and reaching beyond the normally brief duration of office of most elected governments, a kind of European-Japanese-American establishment. Attention can be focussed on matters that go beyond the bounds of national interests and exceed periods of legislation.'[53]

Quite so. The interests of nation states, for example your and my interests, are to go by the board; long-term strategies are not the concern of short-lived governments. For these, of course, one needs the Council on Foreign Relations (founded in 1921), the Bilderbergers (founded in 1954) or, as just mentioned, the Trilateral Commission (founded in 1973) out of which those short-lived governments then emerge.

It was none other than that notorious hawk and reported warmonger Zbigniew Brzezinski who had the idea of founding the Trilateral Commission. 'He had just spent a study year in Tokyo and had returned home with the conviction that Japan – "a delicate, endangered flower" – must be incorporated within the transatlantic community of Europeans and North Americans... Shortly thereafter Brzezinski and Rockefeller met at a Bilderberg Conference, that institution where the elites of Western Europe and America had already been practising unrestrained debate about crucial mutual problems for two decades. On their return flight they consolidated their ideas concerning the decision to found a Bilderberg extended to include Japan.'[54]

'Trilateralism can be defined as the project of developing an organic (or relatively permanent) alliance between the major capitalist states, with the aim of promoting (or sustaining) a stable form of world order which is congenial to their dominant interests', wrote the Canadian political scientist Stephen Gill. 'More specifically, this involves a commitment to a more-or-less liberal international economic order.'[55]

'Liberal' here denotes freedom for corporations, not for individual human beings. World trade and commerce is what has to be liberal, i.e. the flow of goods, services and capital. Exactly as it does among the Bilderbergers, 'liberal' denotes 'anything goes'. Everyone sends everything everywhere, without any limitations.

Older readers will remember the peace movement's figure of fear in the 1970s and '80s, Zbigniew Brzezinski. As a security adviser to Carter's administration he made a name for himself as a hardliner who opposed the Soviet Union. Brzezinski is considered to be the begetter of those forces against which the USA is doing battle today and which are striving to plunge the world into a chaos of terror: the Mujahedin, those radical Islamists in Pakistan and Afghanistan. With the help of the CIA, Brzezinski built up the Muslim guerrilla troops in order to drive the Soviet Union out of Afghanistan. The infamous training camps for terrorists were financed by none other than the CIA. Another participant in that undercover war was Osama bin Laden, who thereafter became the world's most-wanted man. In other words, in the figure of bin Laden the USA bred their very own Enemy Number One, in order to use him subsequently as their strategic substitute for the meanwhile defunct Soviet Union. It was essential for them to enable their war machine to continue functioning once the Eastern Bloc had come to an end. Thus it was the alleged strategist of warfare and terror, Brzezinski, who gave birth to the Bilderbergers' baby, the Trilateral Commission.

## Carter's 'trilateral' administration

The media debate about the Trilateral Commission took place, of course, among those attached to the Bilderberg scene. 'The Tri- lateral Commission was just what those who sniff out conspiracies all over the place were waiting for', wrote Bilderberger Theo Som- mer in 1977 in the already mentioned article in *Die Zeit*, which is represented more than any other news medium among that glob- alist club: 'Isn't that where, behind the scenes, the course is set for the decisive direction of world politics? Does that group not have a policy stipulating that as many members as possible should participate in setting the course? Is this not perhaps a clandestine super-government of the western world?'

What nonsense. Surely in a democratic world the one who governs is — well, who? The voter, of course! He or she alone decides who shall govern. Apart, perhaps, from the Bilderbergers and the Trilateral Commission. Having only just been set up by the Bilderbergers, the latter immediately set about conducting its own 'staffing policy' by creating an entire US administration, namely that of Jimmy Carter (US President from 1977 to 1981). 'It cannot be denied', even Bilderberger Theo Sommer has to admit, 'that nineteen leading positions in the Carter administration are held by former "Trilaterals", among them the President himself, his security adviser Brzezinski, Vice-President Mondale, Secretary of State Vance, and Defence Secretary Brown.' And that is not all. There were 'submarines' from the Bilderberg offshoot in the German government as well: 'Two German members also successfully made the leap into ministerial positions: Herbert Ehrenberg and Count Lambsdorff.'

### A minister changes sides

Although Sommer immediately added that 'this was, however, not an attempt at puppeteering'. Of course it wasn't. Perhaps except for the fact that Bilderberger and Trilateral member Count Otto Lambsdorff (FDP) was not just any government minister. He made history and determined the history of his country to a much greater extent than any other minister. It is to Count Otto Lambsdorff that we owe the end of the social-liberal era in 1983 and the subsequent government of Kohl. In short, Lambsdorff has on his conscience the now much-liked former Chancellor Helmut Schmidt while also having inflicted thick-skinned Helmut Kohl on the republic. On 9 September 1982 Lambsdorff, Economics Minster at the time, presented the Federal Chancellor Helmut Schmidt out of the blue with a series of neo-liberal demands in which he slaughtered so many of the Social Democrats' holy cows that the SPD was obliged to terminate the SPD-FDP coalition. Lambsdorff knew this would happen. His central points included a reduction in social benefits together with tax breaks for commerce and for the rich. In other words the list of demands was gauntlet and divorce document all in one. On 17 September 1982, Chancellor Helmut Schmidt announced to the Federal Government that he had lost confidence in his coalition partner. On 1 October 1982 the FDP and the Union toppled Schmidt by means of a constructive vote of no confidence and elected Kohl as Chancellor. Thus did Bilderberger and Trilateral member Lambsdorff guillotine the social-liberal coalition at a stroke. And this of course had absolutely nothing to do with the fact that the grand old man, *spiritus rector* and honorary chairman of the FDP, Walter Scheel (Federal German President from 1974 to 1979), was at that time Chairman of the Bilderbergers. While he was still Federal President, Scheel had received 'trilateral' US President Jimmy Carter for a state visit. We like to remain among ourselves, do we not! Scheel was also President of the European Union, President of the German Council of the European Movement, Honorary President of the German-British Society and – how could it be otherwise – Honorary Doctor at Georgetown (Jesuit) University.

### If not corruptible, then perhaps forgetful?

And what became of Otto Count Lambsdorff's draft for change? He is supposed to have written it because those requirements would have to be put into practice without delay. He could simply not proceed with the social-liberal coalition with a good conscience if this 'Otto list' were not put into practice. And yet: Although all the FDP ministers of the social-liberal coalition (Genscher, Ertl, Lambsdorff) remained in office under Kohl (with the exception of the liberal Interior Minister Gerhart Rudolf Baum, who has since been endeavouring to block non-constitutional projected laws by means of constitutional challenges), the conscientious Count has evidently lost all interest in his demands. 'Quite soon after the 1982/83 change of government there was no longer any decisive or courageous implementation of the draft', we read on the website of the Friedrich-Naumann-Stiftung, which is close to the FDP.

By the way, Lambsdorff was not able to enjoy his successful change of sides for very long. Only one year later, on 29 November 1983, in connection with the Flick affair, the Bonn Prosecution Service accused him and others of corruption. The suspicion was that, in connection with a share transaction, Lambsdorff had exempted the Flick concern of tax commitments, an action for which they rewarded him with several counts of 30,000 marks. On 27 June 1984, when the charge was about to be heard in court, Lambsdorff resigned as Trade and Industry Secretary. He was not, however, convicted of corruption but merely of not having paid tax on the money he had received. Ah, well. So he was not corrupt but merely somewhat forgetful. But he retained his criminal record anyway.

# A global government or not?

Let us return to the Bilderbergers and the Trilateral Commission. Is it, then, a matter of a global government or not? One important clue might lie in the answer to the question: Who would pay for such an institution? Would it be the participants themselves? That would indicate a private affair. Or the countries involved? The German Federal Government, for example, is paid for by the country it governs, i.e. Germany and its taxpayers. It is typical of a government that it involves the country and its taxpayers in covering its costs. Bilderberger Theo Sommer tells us that the Trilateral Commission's bills are not paid by Rockefeller. As is customary among capitalists, he gets *others* to pay for *his* institutions. Bilderberg apologist Theo Sommer states that 'every country' contributes 'its share, which is calculated in accordance with its gross national product'. This would indicate that the Trilateral Commission is financed out of contributions from its 'member states' and that it levies taxes appropriate to each gross national product, an obvious character-istic of a government.

The Bilderbergers, too, have repeatedly been described as a glo-bal government or a kind of global government. As in the case of the Trilateral Commission, three criteria are crucial to discovering whether the Bilderbergers really are a global government:

1.  their global significance,
2.  their political level,
3.  the possible financing of the set-up by taxing the participating countries of origin.

The first two criteria are relatively easy to explain. In view of the top-class membership, their influence, and their supra-continental strategic ambitions, the Bilderbergers clearly span the globe as a whole. They are also clearly transnational in that they supersede regional national associations such as the European Union. Rather than being a global government in an administrative, management sense, the Bilderbergers are like a strategic brain which is capable of anticipating concepts and developments that can later be put into practice by the administrative parts of the global government such as the EU, NATO, GATT, NAFTA, UNO and so on.

But what can be said of the third criterion: Who pays for the cost of these institutions?

Bad news Number 1: initially the CIA
Bad news Number 2: therefore, all of us

'Indirectly the costs of the first Bilderberg Conference at Ooster-beek in 1954 were borne by the US foreign intelligence agency, the CIA', wrote Andreas von Rétyi in his book about the Bilder-bergers:

> The money flowed into the organization partly via Retinger's contacts. But actually the costs of the clandestine conferences are for the most part paid by those who are not supposed to know anything about them: the taxpayers. The country in which a conference takes place also covers costs including most of the security of the guests. Participants themselves pay only for travel and board, which is unlikely to incon-venience many of them. In spite of this, many of those poten-tates have offloaded their expenses on to others. German politicians, for example, expected the relevant parliaments to pay; or else they combined more or less interesting Bilder-berg weekends with a study tour. The end result was that the taxpayer forked out.[56]

And that's how it is. On the internet portal abgeordnetenwatch.de, long-standing Bilderberger Eckart von Klaeden (CDU) replied to a citizen's question: 'My expenses were paid by the German Federal Parliament.' In other words by the German taxpayer. In plain language this means that the Bilderbergers' countries of origin or the organizations employing them are indirectly taxed for the financing of the conferences. The three essential criteria for a global government are thus fulfilled.

But there is also another factor which cannot meet with our approval: this global government conducts its meetings in secret. Firstly this is a denial and a hushing-up of its character as a global government. And secondly it very effectively prevents any kind of reporting about the 'regulational' processes to which it adheres, i.e. how discussion is handled and how opinions are formed among the Bilderbergers and what political actions result therefrom. In other words, monarchs like the corrupt Prince Bernhard and shady characters like Joseph Retinger have founded an international 'talking shop' in which citizens can have no say, either in the decisions reached or in the resulting political measures taken. It is perfectly obvious that both upfront (as in the cases of the Treaties of Rome or the Four Power Agreement) and implicit decisions do arise from Bilderberg Conferences. If this were not the case, such conferences would not take place. Heavyweight conferences of this kind, in which NATO General Secretaries and Presidents of the EU Commission participate, cannot help but have a bearing on international politics. And conversely, no participant can avoid being influenced. That is why elected politicians have no place at such conferences.

## A form of conspiracy

And this is in no way the opinion of outsiders only. In the USA there is even a law against this form of conspiracy. The very aspect which the Bilderbergers claim to be in operation, i.e. a 'private exchange of opinions' among high-ranking persons, is problematical for US citizens, at all events when it is a matter of those high-ranking participants being representatives of foreign governments. It might even be that all the US citizens who have thus far participated in the meetings have made themselves punishable by law, namely in accordance to the 1799 Logan Act which was most recently updated in the 1990s. It says there:

> Any citizen of the United States, wherever he may be, who, without authority of the United States, directly or indirectly commences or carries on any correspondence or intercourse with any foreign government or any officer or agent thereof, with intent to influence the measures or conduct of any foreign government or of any officer or agent thereof, in relation to any disputes or controversies with the United States, shall be fined under this title or imprisoned not more than three years, or both.

This may sound rather complicated, but the intention of the law is perfectly clear: Only the government, and none other, shall have dealings with foreign governments. All those who open up adjacent channels for specific purposes are liable for punishment. And why, to date, has no Bilderberger been punished in accordance with this law? Probably because 'intercourse' or 'correspondence' with foreign governments alone is insufficient. Both must take place 'with intent to influence the measures or conduct of any foreign government or of any officer or agent thereof, in relation to any disputes or controversies with the United States'. And this is an intent which it would be very difficult to prove. To guarantee this it would also be important to

> maintain the secrecy of the conferences and the obscure and generalized formulations in the papers and indeed in the speeches given during conferences.

An American Bilderberger revealing an intention to influence a representative of a foreign government in the above sense would, at that precise moment, possibly be making himself punishable in accordance with the Logan Act.

## A form of government

In order to find an answer to the question as to whether the Bilderbergers are a global government or whether they are intending to form one, it would of course also be useful to refer to what members and guests themselves have said.

Take David Rockefeller. By now his liaison with the Bilderbergers has lasted for over half a century, a period of time after which married couples celebrate their golden wedding. Is there (perhaps with the exception of his wife) anything else in Rockefeller's life that has accompanied him as regularly as this, and virtually without interruption? It's unlikely. So one might assume that the Bilderberg Conferences, or rather the Bilderberg process, would be rather frequently mentioned in his memoirs. Remarkably, however, among 700 pages, there are only three references to them. And surely even that chapter has only been included because otherwise the secrecy issue would have become all too obvious, since as time has gone on too many people have come to know about them and about the central part played in them by Rockefeller. So he couldn't avoid at least mentioning the subject, albeit with as little emphasis as possible, thus giving the impression that the conferences played only a marginal role in his life. And yet even his first paragraph makes it clear that in reality he is keen to debunk any 'conspiracy theories' which may surround the Bilderberg Conferences. They would have to 'induce apocalyptic visions of omnipotent international bankers plotting with unscrupulous government officials to impose cunning schemes on an ignorant and unsuspecting world', he conjectures (p.372).

It is a mistake to conclude that Rockefeller would vehemently deny this. He merely contradicts it in what amounts to an innocuous version of those suppositions: 'The truth is that Bilderberg is really an intensely interesting annual discussing group that debates issues of a significance to both Europeans and North America – without reaching consensus.' (p.411) That may be so, but of course a consensus need not involve all those present. What matters is a consensus between the important persons involved in each case. Rockefeller then goes on to report that the conference was convened by Prince Bernhard of the Netherlands and Joseph Retinger, 'a Pole of aristocratic origins who had served with British intelligence during World War II'. But how did Retinger, who is unknown to almost all ordinary mortals, manage to convene such a round of heavyweights? 'Retinger, a dynamic and energetic man who spoke with a heavy accent and walked with a pronounced limp, was concerned about the tense relations within the Atlantic community. He persuaded Bernhard to convene a group of prominent individuals to discuss these matters.'[57]

Sure: You're a bit worried and think it might be a good idea if a few people could talk about things, so right away you convene an international conference from among the upper echelons of global society — it's that easy. But I would like to bet that the really important thing is *who* exactly is a bit worried if someone like Rockefeller is expected to come swanning across the Atlantic with a further dozen top Americans and, furthermore, not without having packed his homework in his luggage. For Retinger had 'asked me to prepare a background paper on prospects for the world economy from the American perspective'. Whereupon the multi-billion-dollar oil baron promptly sharpened his pencil while wondering whether what he could produce would satisfy the expectations of Retinger and the other conference participants. But what — apart from his secret service work — made that fabled Mr Retinger so different from 'ordinary' contemporaries whom Rockefeller would certainly not have been so anxious to please? No doubt it was the fact, not mentioned by Rockefeller at this point, that above all else Retinger was a practising Jesuit, and perhaps indeed a Jesuit monk well experienced in playing games of intrigue and networking at the highest level.

Interestingly, though, Rockefeller is not at all consistent in his memoirs. Elsewhere, disarmingly honest statements slip out which contradict the way he downplays his role and his plans. He refers to 'ideological extremists' some of whom 'believe we are part of a secret cabal working against the best interests of the United States, characterizing my family and me as "internationalists" and accusing us of conspiring with others around the world to build a more integrated global and political structure – one world, if you will'.[58] Well, what Rockefeller denounces as the overblown ideas of those 'ideological extremists' do actually amount to very serious accusations:

– 'part of a secret cabal working against the best interests of the United States',
– conspiring with others to 'build a more integrated global and political structure'.

And whereas for the most part Rockefeller very much downplays his own role and that of his organizations, he now suddenly bursts out with: 'If that's the charge, I stand guilty, and I am proud of it.' A secret plot against the United States, conspiracy to establish a global structure – and he's proud of it? This really does look as though Rockefeller would be a prime candidate for an indictment or a judicial enquiry on the basis of the Logan Act. Once in a while the genuine Rockefeller does indeed emerge from all that politically correct fog.

His memoirs also contain only a few pages on the Trilateral Commission founded by the Bilderbergers, pages which contain a good deal of disinformation. He claims, for example, that Jimmy Carter's administration was not 'government by the Trilaterals'. He distances himself very thoroughly from Jimmy Carter, calling him an 'obscure Democratic Governor of Georgia' (p.378) without explaining how or why such an 'obscure' man had been chosen for the Trilateral Commission. Rockefeller declares himself to have been 'amazed' that Carter had not only succeeded in being nominated by the Democrats, but also won the Presidency in 1977. Yet as a co-founder of the Trilateral Commission surely Rockefeller must have played some considerable part in that process. In reality, wrote Laurence H. Shoup, David Rockefeller had met with Carter two years before the founding of the Trilateral Commission, together with Hedley Donovan who was at the time managing editor of *Time Magazine* and later became President Carter's chief adviser for internal affairs and the media: 'Carter was consequently no stranger to these national leaders when they decided to form the Trilateral Commission in the Spring of 1973.'[59] According to Will Banyan, Rockefeller was seeking a replacement for the Administration of Gerald Ford, Nixon's successor: 'The alternative President soon emerged in the form of Jimmy Carter, Governor of Georgia. Carter seemed to be the ideal Trilateral candidate; he had been an enthusiastic member of the Trilateral Commission ever since David had personally invited him to join in 1973, attending all of the meetings.'[60]

And lo and behold: Hardly had its Executive Committee met for the very first time when Carter, one week later, announced his candidature to the Democrats' presidential nominating convention. And hardly had Carter become President of the United States when (according to Rockefeller) he had appointed no fewer than fifteen members of the Trilateral Commission (TC) to the most important posts, from the Vice President via the Secretary of State and the Defence Secretary to the Finance Secretary and national security adviser and founder of the TC, Zbigniew Brzezinski. 'Quite a surprise', wrote Rockefeller in all seriousness in his memoirs.[61] According to Will Banyan, Rockefeller is, even here, only telling half the truth. In reality, 26 members of Carter's Administration were former members of the Trilateral Commission; however, prior to accepting government posts the 'Trilaterals' usually withdrew from membership.[62] 'All we need', Rockefeller is quoted as saying at a meeting of the United Nations Economic Committee on 14 September 1994, 'is a really big crisis, and the nations will accept the new world order'.[63]

A crisis? Let's see: Might this not be the very crisis we are at present

– since 2007 – experiencing? Has this crisis perhaps been staged for the very purpose of setting up the world government? Is this 'new world order' intended to end with a formal global government?

## Long live the crisis

There is indeed much to show that on the whole the global Bilderberg strategists welcome the financial crisis because

– it is destroying the current political order and structure and
– will either make the installation of a new political world order easier, or may even force it into existence.

Is this mere fantasy? Or a conspiracy theory? Certainly not. For the Bilderbergers the financial crisis is plainly 'The Chance for a New World Order', as Henry Kissinger entitled an article on 12 January 2009: 'As the new U.S. administration prepares to take office amidst grave financial and international crises, it may seem counter-intuitive to argue that the very unsettled nature of the international system generates a unique opportunity for creative diplomacy.' (see henryakissinger.com)

Kissinger sounds almost pleased to point out that although all countries will of course as far as possible seek independence from the conditions that have caused the collapse, nevertheless they will be forced to face up to a reality in which their problems will only be manageable by acting together.

'Current international economic policy seems to be based on the illusion that once the current crisis subsides, the old globalized system can be restored', says Kissinger. But, and this is where it gets interesting, one main reason for the crisis was the imbalance between the economic and the political organization of the world. The financial collapse had revealed the illusion and shown up the lack of global institutions which might cushion the shock and reverse the trend. In plain language this means that while the

Bilderberg members were creating the world-corporation, the political institutions were failing to globalize and create a world state.

All over the world the low-point of the existing international finance system was coming up against a concurrent political crisis. Or, to put it in the clearest terms: 'The alternative to a new international order is chaos.'

There were only two possibilities for harmonizing the political and economic systems: either there would be an 'international political system', i.e. a global government or a global state, or it would be necessary to shrink 'the economic units to a size manageable by existing political structures'. Here it is again – the global corporation as 'the normative force of what already exists'. The economic unit has simply outgrown the capability of national states to cope with it. Either the national states are expanded to form a world state, or there would have to be a process of shrinkage which would be 'likely to lead to a new mercantilism', presumably at a regional level. Once again: either a global state or back to the sixteenth to nineteenth centuries. 'Such a return to mercantilism and nineteenth-century diplomacy would divide the world into competing regional units with dangerous long-term consequences', threatens Kissinger.

He is also delighted to note that 'all the principal actors on the world stage' express the wish to bring about the changes necessitated by the financial crisis in collaboration with the United States. So he sees the influence of the United States extending beyond the realm of its traditional allies. Since the financial crisis was also affecting other 'principal actors' on the world stage, such as Russia and China, they, too, might feel prompted to collaborate with the USA.

### Excursus: Barack and the Bilderbergers

The President of the USA, Barack Obama, who counts among his helpers Zbigniew Brzezinski, Kissinger's friend from the Trilateral

Commission, is likely to play a very special role in all this. 'The extraordinary impact of the president-elect on the imagination of humanity is an important element in shaping a new world order,' writes Henry Kissinger. In other words, charismatic black Barack Obama, who appears to represent several ethnicities and cultural regions simultaneously, certainly did not enter into office by accident. Through his demeanour and presence he is to give a global signal for bringing together as many ethnicities as possible, thus uniting them in a new world order. So one can only superficially regard Barack Obama as an expression of a new liberalism, or as the achievement of a popular movement, or a President elected 'from below'.

Or do you really believe that Mr and Mrs Smith, i.e. ordinary voters, can be permitted to determine who shall be the captain of the great US ship of state which has been sailing around the world since 2001 on a new strategic combat patrol?

Of course not. For it is not Mr and Mrs Smith who want a strategy, a credit crisis or a system of global unity. The current strategic operation is a long-term, geopolitical project which cannot do with interruptions brought on by Mr and Mrs Smith, interruptions such as the unfortunate slip which foolishly brought Bill Clinton into the fray for eight years between George Bush senior and George Bush junior. The so-called Neoconservatives seethed with rage at the delay of the long-planned wars in Afghanistan and Iraq, in the end endeavouring to remove Clinton from his post with the help of a decoy named Monica Lewinsky.

Barack Obama is in reality not a fluke and also not a 'people's President' but the next logical step along the path to the 'New World Order'. So he would be a first-rate candidate for the Bilderbergers. But what do I mean by 'would'? We mentioned the Carter administration having been regarded as an administration of the Trilateral Commission. Well, in the same way the Obama administration is an administration of the Bilderbergers. And Obama, the former Senator from Illinois, is indeed a veritable flyweight by comparison with the Bilderberger heavyweights in his original cabinet:

**Vice-President Joe Biden** is a Bilderberger and member of the Council on Foreign Relations.

**Secretary of State Hillary Clinton** has attended Bilderberg Conferences, is a member of the Council on Foreign Relations and of the Trilateral Commission.

**Defense Secretary Robert Gates** is a member of the Council on Foreign Relations and a Bilderberger.

**Finance Secretary Timothy F. Geithner** is a Bilderberger, a 'Trilateral' and a member of the Council on Foreign Relations. As former President and Business Manager of the Federal Reserve Bank of New York and Director for Politics and Development of the International Monetary Fund, he hails from the very heart of the finance establishment. He is also a colleague in Kissinger Associates.

**Economics Secretary Bill Richardson** is a Bilderberger, a member of the Council on Foreign Relations and also works with Kissinger Associates.

**Lawrence Summers of the National Economic Council** is a Bilderberger and belongs to the Trilateral Commission and the Council on Foreign Relations. During the incumbency of President Clinton he was Finance Secretary and chief economist at the World Bank.

**Obama's economics adviser Paul Volcker** is also a Bilderberger, and is with the Trilateral Commission and the Council on Foreign Relations. During the incumbencies of Carter and Reagan he was Chairman of the Federal Reserve and Geithner's predecessor as President of the Federal Reserve Bank of New York, and also on the board of J. Rothschild Wolfensohn & Co.

**National Security Adviser General James L. Jones** is a Bilderberger and a member of the Trilateral Commission. Together with Zbigniew Brzezinski, Bobby Ray Inman, Bilderberg boss Henry Kissinger and former CIA Director John Deutch, he is also a member of the Institute for International Affairs.

**Secretary for Health Tom Daschle** is a Bilderberger and member of the Council on Foreign Relations.

Quite something. But has Barack Obama actually been present in person at a Bilderberg Conference? There is no official confirmation of this. But they did at least once come close, on 5 June 2008. The 2008 Bilderberg Conference was just beginning at the classy Westfield Marriott Washington Dulles hotel when a plane at Washington Dulles Airport packed with journalists was waiting for presidential candidate Obama, who was to fly to Chicago accompanied by the press. But, strange to say, this did not happen. The doors of the plane were closed, and once the journalists were shut inside they were told that the candidate would not be travelling with them as he was attending a 'private meeting' – the customary formulation for a Bilderberg Conference. The journalists didn't find this at all funny, so the following dispute ensued:

'Why were we not told about this meeting until we were on the plane, the doors were shut and the plane was about to taxi to take off?' a reporter asked Obama's spokesman Robert Gibbs.

'Senator Obama had a desire to do some meetings, others had a desire to meet with him tonight in a private way, and that is what we are doing', replied Gibbs.

'Is there more than one meeting, is there more than one person with whom he is meeting?' asked another reporter.

'I am not going to get into all the details of the meeting', Gibbs replied. (WorldNetDaily – wnd.com – 7.6.2008)

Only one word will do: Bilderberg. But since the press on the plane knew nothing of the conference taking place so close by they were unable to ask any pertinent questions – had they so wished.

'If the President goes bike riding, we go with him', said a reporter. 'If he goes out to dinner or goes to visit a friend three blocks up the road, we go with him in the motorcade. That's the expectation in a general election, and that's the way it's been with previous candidates', one reporter told Gibbs. (See infokrieg.tv, 6.6.2008)

No, that isn't how things are. At least not when the Bilderbergers don't want them to be. It's then perfectly alright for the assembled press to be loaded on to a plane and sent on their way to Chicago while the presidential candidate attends a 'private meeting'. But was he actually with the Bilderbergers or not? That's what Bilderberg researcher Jim Tucker, mentioned earlier, also wanted to know, so he telephoned Obama's campaign office. No-one wanted to talk about it, but no-one wanted to deny his presence at the Bilderbergers either.[64]

## Top Bilderberger Kissinger cheers Obama

'President Obama has come into office at a moment of unique opportunity', rejoiced Kissinger in *The Washington Post* of 22 April 2009. ('Obama's Foreign Policy Challenge') 'The economic crisis absorbs the energies of all the major powers; whatever their differences, all need a respite from international confrontation. Overriding challenges such as energy, the environment and proliferation concern them to a considerable degree and in an increasingly parallel way. The possibility of comprehensive solutions is unprecedented', exults the leading globalist and Bilderberger.

'America and its potential partners', wrote Kissinger in *The Chance for a New World Order*, 'can transform a moment of crisis into a vision of hope.'

His use of the word 'potential' is very significant here. Rather than the current partners, what he means are those who ought to become partners as a consequence of the crisis. That is what's so 'beautiful' about the crisis.

Could the Bilderbergers or circles related to them really have kick-started the financial crisis in order to force the New World Order on to the nations? Could it be that the Bilderbergers or circles close to them have taken the whole world hostage and are aiming their pistol at all of us in order to impose a 'new order'? Is the financial crisis actually a revolution from above?

## 'Motive, means and opportunity' — legal action against the Bilderbergers

As one must, when a crime has been committed, we shall have to ask ourselves the question: Did the accused have a motive, the means and the opportunity to commit the crime? In American law, in addition to substantive proof these three elements are required in order to convince the jury in a trial that the accused is guilty. For example, if he shoots someone at night in a lonely spot in order to rob him of his money, the motive is avarice, the means his weapon and the opportunity the victim's location in a lonely spot.

According to these criteria, the Bilderbergers are highly suspect:

**The motive:** Establishment of a 'One World Order' with a global government. Proof: the Bilderbergers' globalist and antinational statements, their citing of a desire for a new world order and a global government.

**The means:** The entire financial elite of the world was convened by the Bilderbergers, from the World Bank and the International Monetery Fund, via global leading banks such as (temporarily) Rockefeller/Chase Manhattan, Lazard Frères, Rothschild, Deutsche Bank and more, right down to creative investment sharks who have only now developed 'new finance instruments' and fantasy ideals involving untold trillions such as, for example, Henry R. Kravis's 'leveraged buyout'.

**The opportunity:** This 'gang' certainly had the opportunity to trigger and stage-manage the crisis when the international finance system and international politics stood before them in all their vulnerability during the final decade of the twentieth and the early years of the twenty-first century. Neither the bankers nor the politicians had the slightest comprehension of the newfangled financial instruments, deals and derivatives they were inflicting on the people. There was no science of 'toxicology' for the so-called toxic assets. The toxic papers were the biological weapons of the financial system. Inconspicuously and inscrutably they infected the whole system until it collapsed. The opportunity is provided by the widespread cluelessness, defencelessness and, not least, the indifference of the victim. Neither the normal bankers nor the politicians have anything they might set against the global finance strategists and the mathematical avant-garde of investment alchemists. Their gambits and strategies belong in the realms of higher mathematics into which neither decent bankers nor politicians normally venture.

But by the standards of a decent lawsuit there is a lack of any concrete proof for a judgement 'beyond any reasonable doubt': Who can be proved to have entered into agreements with whom for the purpose of destroying the international finance system and erecting a 'New World Order'? Among much else, we do not know what might lie hidden beneath the Bilderbergers' much-quoted vow of silence. But one must assume that such agreements, if ever entered into, were even in that setting not reached within the hearing of all and sundry.

We are now, though, in a better position to assess the information supplied by Bilderberg observer Daniel Estulin. Since he cites anonymous sources from within the 2009 Conference it has been necessary to gain some background information in order better to judge the validity of what he has to say: 'According to Estulin's sources, which have been proven highly accurate in the past, Bilderberg is divided on whether to put into motion "either a prolonged agonizing depression that dooms the world to decades of stagnation, decline and poverty ... or an intense-but-shorter depression that paves the way for a new sustainable economic world order, with less sovereignty but more efficiency".'[65]

According to a report from Canada Free Press, Estulin warns 'that Bilderberg are fostering a false picture of economic recovery, suckering investors into ploughing their money back into the stock market again only to later unleash another massive downturn which will create massive losses and searing financial pain in the months ahead'.[66]

Estulin's sources also tell him that Bilderberg will again attempt to push for the enactment of the Lisbon Treaty ... by forcing the Irish to vote on the document once more in September/October.[67]

And on 2 October 2009 a majority of the Irish population did indeed, on their second attempt, vote in favour of the 'reform agreement'.

In view of all we have meanwhile heard about the Bilderberg Conference and the role it played in the unification of Europe, this does indeed sound all too plausible. In addition, all the information we have about the attitude of the Bilderbergers regarding the financial crisis also points towards an identical outcome. Whether it is Kissinger – as quoted above – or any of the others: basically they are all singing the same song.

Thus World Bank President and Bilderberger Robert Zoellick said in London on the eve of the 2009 G20 Summit (2 April 2009): 'If leaders are serious about creating new global responsibilities *or governance*, let them start by modernising multilateralism to empower the WTO, the IMF, and the World Bank Group *to monitor national policies.*' (financialexpress.com, 1.4.2009)

Creating a new global responsibility 'or governance'? How interesting! To 'modernise' multilateralism in international politics must surely mean, in this instance, to dismantle it bit by bit and replace it with the unilateralism of administrative world organizations intended to keep a closer eye on national measures in future. There is no doubt that a further step of this kind towards a central global government would be in keeping with Kissinger's descriptions.

'We can't leap to world governance in one quick step', said Rockefeller crony and founder of the Trilateral Commission Zbigniew Brzezinski in 1995. This aim 'calls for a process of extending the reach of democratic collaboration in stages … an extension, step by step, stage by stage, stone by stone of the existing relatively narrow zones of stability'.[68]

## The new political system

I have not yet mentioned an interesting, important and even alarming element in Kissinger's article 'The Chance for a New World Order' of 12 January 2009, quoted in detail earlier. When studying the article closely we notice that Kissinger strenuously avoids even hinting at *what kind* of global political order or *what kind* of global political system he actually means. Instead of calling a spade a spade he uses cryptic expressions such as 'a vision of hope', 'creative diplomacy', 'common action', 'a new international order', 'global institutions', 'comprehensive solutions'. In short, he behaves like a blustering door-to-door salesman endeavouring to exploit a customer's problem by foisting some entirely new product on him. What that is, he does not say.

But why not? What might the reason be for doggedly concealing the exact nature of the 'New World Order' from the peoples of the world? Could it be that global strategist Kissinger himself has not the faintest idea what that new order might be? Surely not. There can be no doubt that Kissinger has a very clear idea of the new order. Or is the new order, perhaps, intended to usher in a golden age for all of us? Again unlikely, since in that case why should he make a secret of it? No, the reason for keeping it a secret must surely be that we, the normal citizens, would thoroughly dislike the new order.

Kissinger's lack of precision on this point forces us to follow a different route. There are two ways in which we can reach an idea of the new order:

— The first is to study protagonists such as Kissinger and the other Bilderbergers.
— The second involves embarking on structural considerations.

Let us now take the first path. What kind of new order does Kissinger's political career show us? We remember what the American star journalist Seymour Hersh wrote about Henry Kissinger: '... when the rest of us can't sleep we count sheep, and this guy has to count burned and maimed Cambodian and Vietnamese babies until the end of his life.' Kissinger overthrew a democratically elected president in Chile and watched as a bloodthirsty dictatorship ensued. Actually, human rights organizations hate this winner of the Nobel Peace Prize. Numerous actions have been brought in order to call Kissinger to account for his machinations. Because of pending actions the 'dove of peace' has meanwhile been obliged to stay away from a number of countries. For example he has been accused of being involved in Operation Condor in which several Latin American dictatorships joined to pursue and murder regime opponents. Kissinger is also alleged to have had a hand in the bloody invasion of East Timor by Indonesia in 1975 and 1976. And he is reported to have referred to the Italian Christian Democrat Aldo Moro, who was murdered by the Red Brigade, as 'Italy's Allende' – which sounds almost like a death sentence.

On 14 August 1997 the Greek journal *Oikonomikos Tachydromos* quoted something the holder of the Nobel Peace Prize is alleged to have said (and which Kissinger denies): 'The Greek people are anarchic and difficult to tame', he was reported as saying. 'For this reason we must strike deep into their cultural roots: Perhaps then we can force them to conform. I mean, of course, to strike at their language, their religion, their cultural and historical reserves, so that we can neutralize their ability to develop, to distinguish themselves, or to prevail; thereby removing them as an obstacle to our strategically vital plans in the Balkans, the Mediterranean, and the Middle East.' Kissinger apparently finds fault with the anarchy of the Greeks, i.e. their rejection of being dominated. By complaining about this he is supposedly showing that he is interested in aspiring to 'tame' them. So much for the political implications. This is then followed by a tirade of unbridled hatred against a whole nation whose cultural roots he allegedly wants to destroy by taking it out on their language, their religion and their cultural and historical reserves. According to this report, Kissinger wants to 'neutralize', i.e. destroy, that nation's overall ability to develop, to define and to assert itself. Is this the true visage of that leading Bilderberger? And if Kissinger supposedly talks like this about the Greeks, does he talk and think about other nations in the same vein? After all, while Kissinger's publicly unctuous-sounding platitudes regarding the huge purpose of placing the whole world under a single regime may sound rather mild, a method of proceeding in the manner just described would be way more plausible and effective. In other words: Is it really likely that the globalists want to unite the world by means of empty phrases and soap-box oratory? Or is it rather that the rule of force by the more powerful dominates what goes on behind the scenes?

Kissinger himself, as stated, denies the authenticity of the quote. And not only that: he indignantly disputes it.

*Dear Mr. Wisnewski:*

*The quotation attributed to me is a malicious fabrication that has been repudiated numerous times by me and by many others. They are neither my words nor a reflection of my beliefs. In fact, I have greatest respect for the language, culture and traditions of Greece, the birthplace of art, architecture, literature, law and the first democratic forms of government. It is unthinkable that this monstrous falsehood can still be given any credence. Should you run across it in the future, please feel free to share this letter.*

*Sincerely yours,*
*Henry A. Kissinger*

I am of course delighted to share this letter. But at the same time I do ask myself whether this glowing defence of a culture and a nation does truly represent the genuine opinion of Kissinger, that hegemonic and global strategist.

But let us return to the matter of constructing a New World Order. What was it David Rockefeller was saying? 'All we need is a really big crisis, and the nations will accept the new world order.'

So things are still as they always have been: 'Money rules the world.' However, hitherto this has been taken figuratively. Are we now threatened with a world government of financial jugglers, casino speculators and gone-bust bankers? After all, this is the very group who not only represent a world government but can also conjure it into existence by means of a global crisis. As we know, people should be judged less by their words than by their deeds. And in this sense Rockefeller's super-elite clubs such as the Bilderbergers and the Trilateral Commission speak volumes. There can be absolutely no doubt that Rockefeller backs the super-elites in the matter of leading the world.

But what does a government of this kind actually look like? What is the concept here? A democracy? Hardly. For that would mean a 'leadership by the people'. In reality those individuals are thinking of a pre-democratic, archaic, long-outdated model of a state. Government by a wise elite is reminiscent of the state as conceived of by the Greek philosopher Plato, where erudite philosophers govern the three estates, peasants and craftsmen, watchmen and soldiers, and 'philosopher kings'. These philosopher kings gain their legitimacy solely through their 'wisdom'. But what is wisdom and how is it defined? A closer look soon shows that the concept is utterly arbitrary. Even Adolf Hitler and Heinrich Himmler saw themselves as wise men. In fact every dictator has hitherto claimed this 'wisdom'. And when the people rebelled against such government, that was merely an expression of their lack of wisdom. The definition of wisdom is, of course, determined by 'those who are wise'. In other words, there is no control nor has it any genuine legitimisation; 'wisdom' in whatever form it might take can in reality not represent any legitimacy. So this idea of a state opens every door to dictatorship.

So this elite of 'world bankers' is set to turn history back by 2,500 years. It is the desire of 'world bankers' to snatch power for themselves. And the way they set about it is not at all squeamish: James Warburg, a scion of the global banking dynasty M. M. Warburg & Company, is quoted as saying 'We shall have World Government, whether or not we like it. The only question is whether World Government will be achieved by conquest or consent.'[69]

James Warburg's father, Paul Warburg, was one of the fathers and first directors of America's Federal Reserve System and of the Council on Foreign Relations.

### Power to the philanthropists

Did I mention 'government by philosophers'? Or perhaps by stinking-rich philosophers? Oh dear, no. That would be entirely misleading. What I meant, of course, was government by philanthropists.

Are we not truly 'one world' in which each depends on all the others, however far apart they may reside? Do all these leaders betray nothing but responsibility and far-sightedness as they make plans so diligently for the globe as a whole? Surely we ought to believe what those 'philanthropists' are saying during their globalist meetings: 'Let's leave this conference with all of us believing that each in our own way is the voice of a child, a child waiting to be caressed by someone who cares.' — 'If each and every one of us does this, and if we take this message back to our lands, to our many, many different societies, then truly we will make the twenty-first century a century of greatness, where the wealth of the nations of the world and the wealth of the peoples of the world will increase and we can say we have made it a more perfect world.' This, for example, is what one of those philanthropists said in the year 2000.

One year later, in 2001, the children of Afghanistan became acquainted with the scatter-bombs of those philanthropists, which look like toys and then explode when touched. Three years after that, in 2003, the same philanthropist misled the World Security Council when he claimed that weapons of mass destruction were being stockpiled in Iraq. And in the same year that philanthropist also delighted the children of Iraq with his pretty bomblets that shattered their young lives. This reference is to Colin Powell who was selling the USA's wars of aggression against Afghanistan and Iraq as peace missions. Nowadays far more people are dying in Afghanistan and Iraq than was the case under the old regimes. Afghanistan was transformed into the earth's largest drugs plantation, supplying about 95 per cent of the world's opium requirements (base substance for heroin). The globalists are bursting at the seams with philanthropists and peace doves of this kind.

## An attack on the structure of the globe

The second way in which we can discover what kind of a world is approaching us involves taking the structural route.

All along, commercial initiatives reaching beyond European and trans-Atlantic regions have been praised by the Bilderbergers, for example the reduction of American duty on Japanese goods: 'This was a particularly courageous action since it resulted in a flood of cheap Japanese textiles' on the American market, reads some of this praise expressed during a Bilderberg Conference. (Bilderberg Group, Garmisch-Partenkirchen Conference, op.cit.) Purposely springing a leak on a national economy was sold as a 'courageous action'. Free trade within Europe (the 'Common Market') is only one step on the way to worldwide free trade. It underlines not only the transnational but also the transcontinental character of the Bilderbergers, which in the final result leads to a globalist attitude of mind. Bilderberg policy signifies the complete demolition of all (trade) frontiers together with all the resulting catastrophic consequences, such as abolition of protection for regional and national markets and thus a loss of many millions of jobs, a lowering of wages, a lack of variety in the character and quality of goods and cultures, and also the centralization of government, and much else.

## A regimen of crises

Seen in the abstract this means the abolition of the world's cellular (i.e. national) structure and the transformation of the globe into a single economic, legal, cultural and military body. It would be like tearing down all the bulkheads in a ship's hull. The first small leak would soon fill the whole ship and sink it. The initial inrush of water is already under way: the speed with which the financial crisis has spread around the globe is a direct consequence of that policy. And just as would be the case in a ship without bulkheads, the inrush of water is proving disastrous for the system as a whole. 'The banks have checked out of the financial crisis and are now pre-paring for what will come next', wrote *Spiegel Online* on 8 September 2009. 'One important question is: How can a further collapse of the markets be prevented? It can't, says expert Avinash Persaud; because globalization covers the network as a whole.'

This signifies that the friends of globalization, our politicians in other words, have rendered the world defenceless against crises of every kind. Globalization is being driven forward powerfully by means of crises. One need think only of 11 September 2001, when the whole world became similarly embroiled in an artificially engendered crisis which has brought about further change. As we in Germany know from painful experience, a crisis is an ideal device for the establishment of new regimes. Unlike a positive temptation or a positive 'vision' or utopia, a crisis motivates by means of fear and panic and is thus far more effective. Fear may be an inadequate adviser, but it is certainly a good sales agent, whether for vaccines against swine-flu or for new (global) regimes. Apart from 9/11 one might also mention the climate catastrophe in this connection. This makes it possible for a communal 'climate regime' to be set up which inflicts a centrally planned economy on the world as a whole. $CO_2$ is an ideal substance for this. Since it exists wherever anything moves, all such processes can be interfered with and governed from outside.

From the point of view of structural control, the fathers of the European Union and 'world free trade' are veritable ghost-drivers, aiming to abolish every global security measure. By this means economic crises and unemployment can multiply in the communal space like water leaking into a ship's unprotected hull. Globalist groups such as the Bilderbergers are wilfully chopping down all the national props that give the earth support. For reasons obvious to everyone, the cellular system of national states (think of the ship's hull) provides far greater stability, especially in the economic field, although not only there. Whatever the crisis affecting an individual cell or groups of cells, it cannot then multiply unhindered. But in a globalized world the situation is utterly different.

Serious conflicts between individual cells and groups of cells (World War II) have been cited as justification for chopping down the bulkheads, because the claim was that the very cellular structure itself (i.e. the organization of nations around the world) had been the cause of those devastating conflicts. The establishment of the national cell was especially stigmatized on account of National Socialism. A cell thus came to be seen as something unmentionable and loathsome that must be eliminated whatever the cost. And anyone daring to stand up for the cellular structure is himself stigmatised and automatically branded as a representative of crimes which are, according to current opinion, the result of those cells. To be sure, no-one would consider questioning the cellular structure of the human body merely because criminals and crimes exist. That, of course, would lead to the destruction not only of criminals as such but of humanity as a whole. Yet this is precisely the attitude of globalist think-tanks such as the Bilderbergers. The cell itself is the culprit and so, according to their ideology, in order to prevent further devastating conflicts, all boundaries between cells must be torn down. The only problem is that it is not only local and global society which is organized in cellular fashion; for life itself is founded on cells.

## Away with the boundary

So on what do the cells depend? On boundaries, of course. A boundary or border is the necessary prerequisite for life; without boundaries, neither biological nor social, neither psychological nor commercial life is possible. Without boundaries there can be no 'I', and without an I there can be no identity, and without an identity there can be no interests needing to be either harassed or defended. A more highly organized unit without an I, without an identity or interests, is doomed to die. This is the same for an individual, for a corporation or for a social unit such as a nation state. Every bio-logist, every psychologist and every sociologist can tell us many things about the importance of boundaries; it is only the globalists who stamp on them. By doing so they are stamping on life itself through not only ignoring its imperative laws, but by reversing them outright. The destruction of borders or boundaries, so admired by them, leads directly to the destruction of life, whether it be biological, psychological, social or commercial. Although the chronological sequence would be more likely to take place in reverse:

1. commercial (bankruptcy, loss of turnover)
2. social (unemployment, impoverishment)
3. psychological (existential fear)
4. biological (suicide, starvation, sickness, epidemics, civil war)

When the membrane of a cell is destroyed it can no longer protect itself from its environment, and so it perishes because there is nothing to prevent external influences from entering into it and destroying its internal organization. This is no different in the case of societies and regions organized into national states. The dissolution of borders leads directly to their downfall. By destroying life-supporting structures, humanity is finishing itself off by means of unemployment, famine, conflicts and civil wars.

Imagine some medication or other that would dissolve all cellular membranes. What would become of the body? Its cells would be transformed into sludge and it would die. Representatives of the 'one-world-ideology' have thus fallen prey to the error, or rather the madness, of wanting to save or improve a body (= the world) by dissolving its cells (= nation states). In reality, globalization is a programme of death. It is a structural war against the whole of humanity – with the exception of certain elites who will, all the more thoroughly, separate themselves off from the cellular, or rather the national sludge, because they want to survive. It is of course true that there will never be an ideal association of cells (= body, world). Bodies have always been prone to necroses and diseases. But nowadays, in view of rising unemployment and the financial crisis spreading across the globe like wildfire, and accompanied by the consequent establishment of centralized regimes, we can directly witness the disastrous result that follows the dissolution of borders.

It is easy to prove that what is involved here is a programme involving not commerce but doom, aimed at borders as such. If the intention were merely to create a global region for commerce, then those in power would be satisfied with the dissolution of national boundaries. But they are not. Instead they want to do away with all the important borders between human beings. The next to be dealt with are the boundaries between the sexes and the generations. Transsexuality and gender reassignment, fat reduction and muscle enhancement in women, the levelling of lifestyles and fashion – all this leads to the dissolution of boundaries between the sexes. By means of anti-ageing techniques, plastic surgery and standardization of clothing for the generations, the boundaries between generations are also being blurred and increasingly abolished. The same goes for the boundaries between beauty and ugliness, between the more able and the less able (we are all searching for the super-star) and for other borders as well, such as those between families. Instead of strengthening families, commercial, cultural and social constraints weaken them. Every boundary must fall!

## The masked crisis

Of course, for a crisis to be 'efficient' the dose must be correctly administered. If societies were to collapse into chaos before the achievement of globalization, individual cells would seek to save themselves by recreating new borders and reactivating existing membranes in order to form new boundaries. So the disastrous consequences of globalization are being muted while the public is lulled into a sense of security. Unemployment is disguised by social benefits which will be abolished the moment globalization becomes irreversible. While the number of unemployed in Germany is stated to be three to four million, in fact there are about ten million. There is no doubt that the millions of the unemployed and the socially disadvantaged whose jobs have been relocated overseas are still being supported by relatively generous benefits in order to mask the crisis.

# The mightiest conspiracy on the planet

Thinking all this through to the end leads to the conclusion that the Bilderberg strategies evidence a lack of respect for nations as such, including the American nation. Having already been given a trial run, the global corporation they plan to establish is to become a weapon with which to counteract nation states, surpassing them by means of its international character and size and thus making them appear obsolete and questionable.

Thirty years before the share-holders and personnel of Daimler, Chrysler and even Deutsche Post fell victim to the idea of the global corporation, the concept was already being propagated at Bilderberg Conferences. This is proof enough that geostrategic thinking now takes place in elite groups such as that of the Bilderbergers rather than in government circles. Local governments are now merely administrative instruments lacking any strategic perspective or plan for their own nation. At best a government still has a strategic plan for the political parties supporting it to cover the period until the next election. This in turn means that national governments are having to feel their way blindly through a system of long-term strategies designed by others. National governments can only react to those strategies, rather than stepping forward as bearers of their own strategic interests. National governments function like amateur chess computers playing against a pro-fessional-grade chess computer. I actually believe that it is forbidden for national governments to develop their own global strategies. National governments who possess their own identity and strategies find themselves hated by the ruling geostrategists, as evidenced by Iran and Russia, which have never or only rarely attended a Bilderberg conference. The example of the global cor-poration's strategy demonstrates that such proceedings are, for good reason, kept secret. Groups like the Bilderbergers manifest as planning committees and think-tanks that elaborate designs for the world as it is to be in ten or a hundred years from now. The general public is of course not supposed to know about these in case objections are raised against one strategy or another; they have to be developed on the quiet until the course is set and it is too late for any objection. To expect openness from the Bilderbergers would be like asking a chess master to reveal his next few moves; the game would no longer function, or at least not for the master's immediate opponent.

It appears to be a matter not only of economic but also of ideological, if not religious, strategies. However, the global corporations themselves represent merely a temporary weapon against the nation state. They are only a means to an end. At some point they, too, will be sacrificed along the path to the global state. The dismissal of workers and the ongoing expropriation of share-holders will in the long term deprive also the corporations of their existential basis – because they dismiss their own customers and impoverish their share-holders, thus reducing their spending power. In fact a car manufacturing corporation like Daimler-Chrysler is in effect sacking its own customers when it sacks 14,000 employees; a corporation's employees are, by tradition, its most faithful customers. To have 14,000 fewer direct customers amounts, in reality, to a severe blow against a corporation, or any other corporations involved. At the end of the day the result is not a prosperous world; after all, corporations cannot survive without financially strong customers. The end result will be a monolithic corporation that will eventually metamorphose into a consumption dictatorship of lowest-quality standard goods – see George Orwell's *1984*. So the main factor appears in reality to be not turnover or finance, but the establishment of totalitarian power.

This worldwide dictatorship does not exist as yet, although it is in process of being established in isolated instances. We are already beginning to experience the disastrous effect of border abolition leading to centralization. Worldwide ministries are already being set up, for example the World Health Organization (WHO). And just as, in George Orwell's tale, torture is practised in the 'Ministry of Love' and lying goes on in the 'Ministry of Truth', so is the World Health Organization of the UN concerned not with health but with the destruction of health. In 2009, for example, the WHO recommended the large-scale application of insufficiently tested vaccines against 'swine flu' in order subsequently to observe the effects these would have on human beings. Since almost two hundred states are subject to the dictates of the World Health Organization, that 'Ministry of World Health' exercises virtually absolute power over the health and sickness of the world's population. And, as we will remember, the setting up of the United Nations Organization was a much-favoured project of the Bilderbergers.

It is surely sufficiently clear by now that the Bilderbergers might well represent a clandestine conspiracy for the transformation of our planet. A conspiracy is defined as a clandestine association of at least three persons working towards a secret goal. And when, as we have done, we investigate the personnel, the philosophy and the plans of the Bilderbergers, it most certainly does appear to be a matter of one of the most shocking conspiracies ever seen on our planet.[*]

---

[*]Just after our editorial deadline had passed, *The Guardian* announced on 17.11.2009 that before he could be chosen as President of the EU on 19 November 2009, Herman van Rompuy of Belgium was first obliged to attend a meeting with Bilderberg bosses Henry Kissinger and Étienne Davignon.

The global 'Climate Conference' in Copenhagen in December 2009 was chaired by Denmark's 'Minister of Climate' Connie Hedegaard, another Bilderberg participant.

# Acknowledgements

— Andreas von Rétyi, Daniel Estulin and all the other Bilderberg researchers for their invaluable efforts to enlighten us,
— All the staff at the Plaza Vouliagmeni for their ever-friendly service to, and their patience with, an assorted bunch of international journalists,
— Paul Dorneanu, Giorgio Bombassei, Sybille van Steenberghe, Christoph Klöppner, Salam Mahdi, Bernard Davids and Peter Papaheraklis (especially for organizing the chartered boat),
— Willy Brunner, who accompanied me in my research on one of the chapters,
— And as ever my family for their patience with a frequently very much preoccupied 'top boss'.

# Appendix

## BILDERBERG MEETINGS
P.O.Box 3017          Fax      +31 71 5280 522
2301 DA LEIDEN
The Netherlands

# FAX

| | |
|---|---|
| **Date** | 19 May 2009 |
| **To** | Mr. Marco Elasticfox |
| **Fax #** | +33 3 5901 8861 |
| **Subject** | **Press release** |
| **From** | Maja Banck |
| **Ref #** | 1 |
| **Pages** | 6 |

# *PRESS RELEASE*

### BILDERBERG MEETINGS
### 17 May 2009

The 57th Bilderberg Meeting will be held in Vouliagmeni, Greece 14 – 17 May 2009. The Conference will deal mainly with the financial crisis, governments and markets, role of institutions, market economies and democracies, Iraq, Pakistan and Afghanistan, US and the World, cyberterrorism, new imperialisms, protectionism, post-Kyoto challenges. Approximately 130 participants will attend of whom about two-thirds come from Europe and the balance from North America. About one-third is from government and politics, and two-thirds are from finance, industry, labor, education, and communications. The meeting is private in order to encourage frank and open discussion.

Bilderberg takes its name from the hotel in Holland, where the first meeting took place in May 1954. That pioneering meeting grew out of the concern expressed by leading citizens on both sides of the Atlantic that Western Europe and North America were not working together as closely as they should on common problems of critical importance. It was felt that regular, off-the-record discussions would help create a better understanding of the complex forces and major trends affecting Western nations in the difficult post-war period.
The Cold War has now ended. But in practically all respects there are more, not fewer, common problems - from trade to jobs, from monetary policy to investment, from ecological challenges to the task of promoting international security. It is hard to think of any major issue in either Europe or North America whose unilateral solution would not have repercussions for the other.
Thus the concept of a European-American forum has not been overtaken by time. The dialogue between these two regions is still - even increasingly - critical.

What is unique about Bilderberg as a forum is the broad cross-section of leading citizens that are assembled for nearly three days of informal and off-the-record discussion about topics of current concern especially in the fields of foreign affairs and the international economy; the strong feeling among participants that in view of the differing attitudes and experiences of the Western nations, there remains a clear need to further develop an understanding in which these concerns can be accommodated; the privacy of the meetings, which has no purpose other than to allow participants to speak their minds openly and freely.
In short, Bilderberg is a small, flexible, informal and off-the-record international forum in which different viewpoints can be expressed and mutual understanding enhanced.

Bilderberg's only activity is its annual Conference. At the meetings, no conclusions are reached, no recommendations are made and no policy statements issued. Since 1954, fifty-six conferences have been held. The names of the participants are made available to the press. Participants are chosen for their experience, their knowledge, and their standing; all participants attend Bilderberg in a private and not an official capacity.

There will be no press conference. A list of participants is appended.

17-5-2009

> **BILDERBERG MEETINGS**
> Vouliagmeni, Greece
> 14-17 May 2009
> **FINAL LIST OF PARTICIPANTS**

**Honorary Chairman**

| | | |
|---|---|---|
| BEL | Davignon, Etienne | Honorary Chairman, Bilderberg Meetings; Vice Chairman, Suez-Tractebel |
| | | |
| DEU | Ackermann, Josef | Chairman of the Management Board and the Group Executive Committee, Deutsche Bank AG |
| USA | Alexander, Keith B. | Director, National Security Agency |
| GRC | Alogoskoufis, George | Member of Parliament |
| USA | Altman, Roger C. | Chairman, Evercore Partners Inc. |
| GRC | Arapoglou, Takis | Chairman and CEO, National Bank of Greece |
| TUR | Babacan, Ali | Minister of State and Deputy Prime Minister |
| GRC | Bakoyannis, Dora | Minister of Foreign Affairs |
| NOR | Baksaas, Jon Fredrik | President and CEO, Telenor Group |
| PRT | Balsemão, Francisco Pinto | Chairman and CEO, IMPRESA, S.G.P.S.; Former Prime Minister |
| | | |
| FRA | Baverez, Nicolas | Partner, Gibson, Dunn & Crutcher LLP |
| ITA | Bernabè, Franco | CEO, Telecom Italia S.p.A. |
| SWE | Bildt, Carl | Minister of Foreign Affairs |
| SWE | Björklund, Jan | Minister for Education; Leader of the Liberal Party |
| CHE | Blocher, Christoph | Former Swiss Counselor; Former Chairman and CEO, EMS-Group |
| | | |
| FRA | Bompard, Alexandre | CEO, Europe 1 |
| USA | Boot, Max | Jeane J. Kirkpatrick Senior Fellow for National Security Studies, Council on Foreign Relations |
| | | |
| AUT | Bronner, Oscar | Publisher and Editor, Der Standard |
| FRA | Castries, Henri de | Chairman of the Management Board and CEO, AXA |
| ESP | Cebrián, Juan Luis | CEO, PRISA |
| BEL | Coene, Luc | Vice Governor, National Bank of Belgium |
| USA | Collins, Timothy C. | Senior Managing Director and CEO, Ripplewood Holdings, LLC |
| | | |
| GRC | David, George A. | Chairman, Coca-Cola H.B.C. S.A. |
| GBR | Dearlove, Richard | Master, Pembroke College, Cambridge |
| GRC | Diamantopoulou, Anna | Member of Parliament |
| ITA | Draghi, Mario | Governor, Banca d'Italia |
| USA | Eberstadt, Nicholas N. | Henry Wendt Scholar in Political Economy, American Enterprise Institute for Public Policy Research |
| | | |
| DNK | Eldrup, Anders | President, DONG A/S |
| ITA | Elkann, John | Chairman, EXOR S.p.A.; Vice Chairman, Fiat S.p.A. |
| DEU | Enders, Thomas | CEO, Airbus SAS |
| ESP | Entrecanales, José Manuel | Chairman, Acciona |
| AUT | Faymann, Werner | Federal Chancellor |
| USA | Ferguson, Niall | Laurence A. Tisch Professor of History, Harvard University |
| IRL | Gleeson, Dermot | Chairman, AIB Group |
| USA | Graham, Donald E. | Chairman and CEO, The Washington Post Company |

17-5-2009

| | | |
|---|---|---|
| NLD | Halberstadt, Victor | Professor of Economics, Leiden University; Former Honorary Secretary General of Bilderberg Meetings |
| NLD | Hirsch Ballin, Ernst M.H. | Minister of Justice |
| USA | Holbrooke, Richard C. | US Special Representative for Afghanistan and Pakistan |
| NLD | Hommen, Jan H.M. | Chairman, ING N.V. |
| INT | Hoop Scheffer, Jaap G. de | Secretary General, NATO |
| USA | Johnson, James A. | Vice Chairman, Perseus, LLC |
| USA | Jordan, Jr., Vernon E. | Senior Managing Director, Lazard Frères & Co. LLC |
| FIN | Katainen, Jyrki | Minister of Finance |
| USA | Keane, John M. | Senior Partner, SCP Partners; General, US Army, Retired |
| USA | Kent, Muhtar | President and CEO, The Coca-Cola Company |
| GBR | Kerr, John | Member, House of Lords; Deputy Chairman, Royal Dutch Shell plc |
| DEU | Klaeden, Eckart von | Foreign Policy Spokesman, CDU/CSU |
| USA | Kleinfeld, Klaus | President and CEO, Alcoa Inc. |
| TUR | Koç, Mustafa V. | Chairman, Koç Holding A.Ş. |
| DEU | Koch, Roland | Prime Minister of Hessen |
| TUR | Kohen, Sami | Senior Foreign Affairs Columnist, Milliyet |
| USA | Kravis, Henry R. | Founding Partner, Kohlberg Kravis Roberts & Co. |
| USA | Kravis, Marie-Josée | Senior Fellow, Hudson Institute, Inc. |
| INT | Kroes, Neelie | Commissioner, European Commission |
| GRC | Kyriacopoulos, Ulysses | Chairman and Board member of subsidiary companies of the S&B Group |
| FRA | Lagarde, Christine | Minister for the Economy, Industry and Employment |
| INT | Lamy, Pascal | Director General, World Trade Organization |
| PRT | Leite, Manuela Ferreira | Leader, PSD |
| ESP | León Gross, Bernardino | General Director of the Presidency of the Spanish Government |
| DEU | Löscher, Peter | CEO, Siemens AG |
| GBR | Mandelson, Peter | Secretary of State for Business, Enterprise & Regulatory Reform |
| INT | Maystadt, Philippe | President, European Investment Bank |
| CAN | McKenna, Frank | Former Ambassador to the US |
| GBR | Micklethwait, John | Editor-in-Chief, The Economist |
| FRA | Montbrial, Thierry de | President, French Institute for International Relations |
| ITA | Monti, Mario | President, Universita Commerciale Luigi Bocconi |
| ESP | Moratinos Cuyaubé, Miguel A. | Minister of Foreign Affairs |
| USA | Mundie, Craig J. | Chief Research and Strategy Officer, Microsoft Corporation |
| CAN | Munroe-Blum, Heather | Principal and Vice Chancellor, McGill University |
| NOR | Myklebust, Egil | Former Chairman of the Board of Directors SAS, Norsk Hydro ASA |
| DEU | Nass, Matthias | Deputy Editor, Die Zeit |
| NLD | Netherlands, H.M. the Queen of the | |
| ESP | Nin Génova, Juan María | President and CEO, La Caixa |
| FRA | Olivennes, Denis | CEO and Editor in Chief, Le Nouvel Observateur |
| FIN | Ollila, Jorma | Chairman, Royal Dutch Shell plc |
| GBR | Osborne, George | Shadow Chancellor of the Exchequer |
| FRA | Oudéa, Frédéric | CEO, Société Générale |
| ITA | Padoa-Schioppa, Tommaso | Former Minister of Finance; President of Notre Europe |
| GRC | Papahelas, Alexis | Journalist, Kathimerini |

2

17-5-2009

| | | |
|---|---|---|
| GRC | Papalexopoulos, Dimitris | Managing Director, Titan Cement Co. S.A. |
| GRC | Papathanasiou, Yannis | Minister of Economy and Finance |
| USA | Perle, Richard N. | Resident Fellow, American Enterprise Institute for Public Policy Research |
| BEL | Philippe, H.R.H. Prince | |
| PRT | Pinho, Manuel | Minister of Economy and Innovation |
| INT | Pisani-Ferry, Jean | Director, Bruegel |
| CAN | Prichard, J. Robert S. | President and CEO, Metrolinx |
| ITA | Prodi, Romano | Chairman, Foundation for Worldwide Cooperation |
| FIN | Rajalahti, Hanna | Managing Editor, Talouselämä |
| CAN | Reisman, Heather M. | Chair and CEO, Indigo Books & Music Inc. |
| NOR | Reiten, Eivind | President and CEO, Norsk Hydro ASA |
| CHE | Ringier, Michael | Chairman, Ringier AG |
| USA | Rockefeller, David | Former Chairman, Chase Manhattan Bank |
| USA | Rubin, Barnett R. | Director of Studies and Senior Fellow, Center for International Cooperation, New York University |
| TUR | Sabanci Dinçer, Suzan | Chairman, Akbank |
| CAN | Samarasekera, Indira V. | President and Vice-Chancellor, University of Alberta |
| AUT | Scholten, Rudolf | Member of the Board of Executive Directors, Oesterreichische Kontrollbank AG |
| USA | Sheeran, Josette | Executive Director, UN World Food Programme |
| ITA | Siniscalco, Domenico | Vice Chairman, Morgan Stanley International |
| ESP | Solbes, Pedro | Vice-President of Spanish Government; Minister of Economy and Finance |
| ESP | Spain, H.M. the Queen of | |
| USA | Steinberg, James B. | Deputy Secretary of State |
| INT | Stigson, Björn | President, World Business Council for Sustainable Development |
| GRC | Stournaras, Yannis | Research Director, Foundation for Economic and Industrial Research (IOBE). |
| IRL | Sutherland, Peter D. | Chairman, BP plc and Chairman, Goldman Sachs International |
| INT | Tanaka, Nobuo | Executive Director, IEA |
| GBR | Taylor, J. Martin | Chairman, Syngenta International AG |
| USA | Thiel, Peter A. | President, Clarium Capital Management, LLC |
| DNK | Thorning-Schmidt, Helle | Leader of The Social Democratic Party |
| DNK | Thune Andersen, Thomas | Partner and CEO, Maersk Oil |
| AUT | Treichl, Andreas | Chairman and CEO, Erste Group Bank AG |
| INT | Trichet, Jean-Claude | President, European Central Bank |
| GRC | Tsoukalis, Loukas | President of the Hellenic Foundation for European and Foreign Policy (ELIAMEP) |
| TUR | Uğur, Agah | CEO, Borusan Holding |
| FIN | Vanhanen, Matti | Prime Minister |
| CHE | Vasella, Daniel L. | Chairman and CEO, Novartis AG |
| NLD | Veer, Jeroen van der | Chief Executive, Royal Dutch Shell plc |
| USA | Volcker, Paul A. | Chairman, Economic Recovery Advisory Board |
| SWE | Wallenberg, Jacob | Chairman, Investor AB |
| SWE | Wallenberg, Marcus | Chairman, SEB |
| NLD | Wellink, Nout | President, De Nederlandsche Bank |

3

17-5-2009

| | | |
|---|---|---|
| NLD | Wijers, Hans | Chairman, AkzoNobel NV |
| GBR | Wolf, Martin H. | Associate Editor & Chief Economics Commentator, The Financial Times |
| USA | Wolfensohn, James D. | Chairman, Wolfensohn & Company, LLC |
| USA | Wolfowitz, Paul | Visiting Scholar, American Enterprise Institute for Public Policy Research |
| INT | Zoellick, Robert B. | President, The World Bank Group |

**Rapporteurs**

| | | |
|---|---|---|
| GBR | Bredow, Vendeline von | Business Correspondent, The Economist |
| GBR | McBride, Edward | Business Editor, The Economist |

| | | | | |
|---|---|---|---|---|
| AUT | Austria | | GRC | Greece |
| BEL | Belgium | | INT | International |
| CHE | Switzerland | | IRL | Ireland |
| CAN | Canada | | ITA | Italy |
| DEU | Germany | | NOR | Norway |
| DNK | Denmark | | NLD | Netherlands |
| ESP | Spain | | PRT | Portugal |
| FRA | France | | SWE | Sweden |
| FIN | Finland | | TUR | Turkey |
| GBR | Great Britain | | USA | United States of America |

4

## BILDERBERG MEETINGS

P.O.Box 3017      Fax     +31 71 5280 522
2301 DA LEIDEN
The Netherlands

# FAX

| | |
|---|---|
| **Date** | 19 May 2009 |
| **To** | Mr. Wesznewsky |
| **Fax #** | +49 89 4115 5467 |
| **Subject** | **Press release** |
| **From** | Maja Banck |
| **Ref #** | 1 |
| **Pages** | 6 |

GÜNTER VERHEUGEN

VIZEPRÄSIDENT DER EUROPÄISCHEN KOMMISSION

RUE DE LA LOI 200 · WETSTRAAT 200
B-1049 BRÜSSEL
TEL. 02/298.11.00 - FAX. 02/299.18.27

Brüssel, den 25. Mai 2009
GV/ns D(2009)/512

Herrn
Gerhard Wisnewski
Postfach 140624
D - 80456 München

Sehr geehrter Herr Wisnewski,

vielen Dank für Ihre Anfrage vom 29. April bezüglich meiner Beteiligung an Bilderberg-Konferenzen.

Ich habe nur ein einziges Mal, und das im Auftrag meiner Bundestagsfraktion, an einer solchen Konferenz teilgenommen. Ich weiß nicht mehr genau, wann das war, aber ich weiß noch wo: auf dem Bürgenstock bei Luzern in der Schweiz.

Ich habe aus der Konferenz keinen besonderen Nutzen gezogen und Einladungen zu späteren Konferenzen so lange abgelehnt, bis keine mehr kamen. Meine sehr beschränkte, einmalige Erfahrung mit dieser Einrichtung, zumal sie nicht sehr nachhaltig war, macht es mir unmöglich, Ihren Fragebogen zu beantworten. Ich hoffe, Sie verstehen das.

Mit freundlichen Grüßen

Günter Verheugen

**Dr. Mathias Döpfner**
Vorstandsvorsitzender

**axel springer** ◪

Herrn
Gerhard Wisnewski
Postfach 140624
80456 München

25. Mai 2009

**Bilderberg-Konferenzen**

Sehr geehrter Herr Wisnewski,

Ihr journalistisches Interesse an den Bilderberg-Konferenzen kann ich nachvollziehen.

Bitte haben Sie aber Verständnis, dass ich mich Ihrem umfangreichen Fragenkatalog wegen zahlreicher anderweitiger Verpflichtungen nicht widmen kann.

Mit freundlichen Grüßen

**Axel Springer AG** Axel-Springer-Straße 65, 10888 Berlin
Telefon: +49 (0) 30 25 91-7 77 00, Fax: +49 (0) 30 25 91-7 77 06
mathias.doepfner@axelspringer.de

HENRY A. KISSINGER

October 28, 2009

Dear Mr. Wisnewski:

The quotation attributed to me is a malicious fabrication that has been repudiated numerous times by me and by many others. They are neither my words nor a reflection of my beliefs. In fact, I have greatest respect for the language, culture and traditions of Greece, the birthplace of art, architecture, literature, law and the first democratic forms of government. It is unthinkable that this monstrous falsehood can still be given any credence. Should you run across it in the future, please feel free to share this letter.

Sincerely yours,

Henry A. Kissinger

Mr. Gerhard Wisnewski
g.wisnewski@freenet.de

TWENTY-SIXTH FLOOR · 350 PARK AVENUE · NEW YORK, NEW YORK 10022 · (212) 759-7919
FACSIMILE (212) 759-0042

# DIE ZEIT

WOCHENZEITUNG FÜR POLITIK • WIRTSCHAFT • WISSEN • KULTUR UND Leben

Herrn
Gerhard Wisnewski
Postfach 140 624

80456 München

**Dr. Josef Joffe**
Herausgeber
Tel. 040-32 80 584
Fax 040-32 80 596

Hamburg, 28. Mai 2009

Sehr geehrter Herr Wisnewski,

ich glaube kaum, dass irgend jemand, der Bilderberg wirklich kennt, Ihnen Ihre Fragen beantwortet hat. Bilderberg ist vertraulich, sonst gäbe es dort keine freie Aussprache.

Weitere Briefe werden nicht beantwortet.

Mit freundlichen Grüßen

Josef Joffe

*Zeitverlag Gerd Bucerius GmbH & Co.*
DIE ZEIT, Pressehaus, Speersort 1, 20095 Hamburg · Telefon: 040 / 32 80-0 · Telefax: 040 / 32 71 11

**Dr. Helmut Kohl**
Bundeskanzler a.D.

- Der Leiter des Büros -

10117 Berlin, den 8. Oktober 2009
Deutscher Bundestag
Unter den Linden 71
Telefon (030) 227 – 73761
Telefax (030) 227 – 76840

Herrn
Gerhard Wisnewski
Postfach 140 624
80456 München

Sehr geehrter Herr Wisnewski,

vielen Dank für Ihr Schreiben vom 18. September 2009 an Herrn Bundeskanzler
a. D. Dr. Helmut Kohl. Er hat mich beauftragt, Ihnen zu antworten.

Sie bitten ihn im Zusammenhang mit Ihrem Buchprojekt über die sog. Bilderberg-
Konferenzen um die Beantwortung mehrerer Fragen.

Herr Bundeskanzler bekommt eine Vielzahl ähnlicher Schreiben, in denen um seine
konkrete Erinnerung nachgesucht wird. Diese Wünsche kann er aber nicht
annähernd erfüllen. Deshalb bitte ich um Verständnis, dass Herr Bundeskanzler auch
Ihrer Bitte nicht entsprechen kann.

Mit freundlichen Grüßen

Dr. Ulrich Pohlmann

 Bundesministerium
des Innern

Freiheit
Einheit
Demokratie

RD Dr. Christian Klos
Leiter Ministerbüro

Bundesministerium des Innern, 11014 Berlin

Herrn
Gerhard Wisnewski
Postfach 14 06 24
80456 München

| | |
|---|---|
| HAUSANSCHRIFT | Alt-Moabit 101 D, 10559 Berlin |
| POSTANSCHRIFT | 11014 Berlin |
| TEL | +49 (0)30 18 681 - 1904 |
| FAX | +49 (0)30 18 681 - 1018 |
| E-MAIL | MB@bmi.bund.de |
| INTERNET | www.bmi.bund.de |

DATUM   Berlin, den 8. Mai 2009

Sehr geehrter Herr Wisnewski,

Bundesminister Dr. Schäuble dankt Ihnen für Ihr Schreiben vom 29. April 2009. Er hat mich gebeten, darauf zu antworten und um Verständnis zu bitten, dass er es terminlich leider nicht einrichten kann, an Ihrem Buchprojekt mitzuwirken und hierzu den von Ihnen übermittelten Fragenkatalog zu beantworten. Ihrem Vorhaben wünscht Herr Minister Dr. Schäuble den erhofften Erfolg.

Mit freundlichen Grüßen

ZUSTELL- UND LIEFERANSCHRIFT   Alt-Moabit 101 D, 10559 Berlin
VERKEHRSANBINDUNG   S-Bahnhof Bellevue; U-Bahnhof Turmstraße
Bushaltestelle Kleiner Tiergarten

**Büro Helmut Schmidt**
- Bundeskanzler a.D. -

Deutscher Bundestag
Platz der Republik 1

11011 Berlin

Tel.: 040 – 5311 761
Fax: 040 – 5273 2209

25. September 2009

Herrn
Gerhard Wisnewski
Postfach 140624
80456 München

Sehr geehrter Herr Wisnewski,

Herr Bundeskanzler a.D. Helmut Schmidt hat Ihren Brief vom 17. August 2009 erhalten und mich gebeten, Ihnen zu danken. Herr Schmidt bittet um Verständnis dafür, daß er wegen allgemeiner Überlastung Ihrer Bitte, Fragen zu den Bilderberg-Konferenzen zu beantworten, leider nicht nachkommen kann.

Mit freundlichen Grüßen

*A. Bazzato*

Andrea Bazzato

**Martin Biesel**
Leiter des Büros des
Vorsitzenden der FDP-Bundestagsfraktion

Herrn
Gerhard Wisnewski
Postfach 140624

80456 München

Berlin, 7. Mai 2009
Ni

Sehr geehrter Herr Wisnewski,

haben Sie vielen Dank für Ihr Schreiben vom 29. April an Herrn Dr. Westerwelle.
Herr Dr. Westerwelle hat mich gebeten, Ihnen zu antworten.

Auf den Bilderberg-Konferenzen treffen sich regelmäßig Teilnehmer aus den
verschiedenen Bereichen von Gesellschaft, Wirtschaft und Wissenschaft. Neben
Fragen der Weltwirtschaft werden vor allem die internationalen Beziehungen
besprochen. Die ca. 120 Teilnehmer werden so ausgewählt, dass eine
ausgeglichene Diskussion über vorgegebene Tagesordnungspunkte stattfinden
kann.

Nochmals vielen Dank für Ihre Zuschrift. Ihnen persönlich alles Gute.

Mit freundlichen Grüßen

Büro Dr. Guido Westerwelle, MdB
Deutscher Bundestag – Platz der Republik 1 – 11011 Berlin
Tel.: 030/227-71636 – Fax: 030/227-76562
Guido.Westerwelle@Bundestag.de
http://www.guido-westerwelle.de

# Notes

1. Publisher: Public Affairs at Perseus, 288 pages, ISBN 0-316-85545-6, publication date: 30 April 2002.
2. Will Banyan: *The Proud Internationalist – The Globalist Vision of David Rockefeller*, (pdf) 2006, p. 67d.
3. You can listen to this report at http://alles-schallundrauch.blogspot.com/2009/05/ bericht-uber-bilderberg-152.html
4. *Handbuch zur ökonomischen Bildung*, publ. Hermann May, Munich/ Vienna 2002, p. 303.
5. *Albers*, ibid., p. 304.
6. Estulin, p. 25f in the German edition.
7. Ibid., p. 26f.
8. Rétyi, p. 44.
9. Ibid., p. 45.
10. Ibid., p. 33.
11. Nexus Magazine, Vol. 3 (1), quoted from Philip Gardiner *Secret Societies: Gardiner's Forbidden Knowledge*, Franklin Lakes, 2007, p. 216.
12. Ibid., p. 63 and 36.
13. Fülöp-Miller, p. 56.
14. Ibid., p. 57.
15. Ibid., p. 60.
16. Ibid., p. 250.
17. Ibid., p. 253.
18. Ibid., p. 254.
19. In ibid., p. 256.
20. Ibid., p. 281.
21. Ibid., p. 283.
22. Ibid.
23. Allen, http://www.sandhed.dk/None-Dare-Call-it-Conspiracy.pdf, p. 12.

24. Fülöp-Miller, p. 7.

25. Ibid., p. 102.

26. Ibid., p. 103.

27. Dr J. H. Retinger, *The Bilderberg Group*, August 1956.

28. See Rockefeller, p. 154.

29. Samuel P. Huntington, *Clash of Civilizations and the Remaking of World Order*, 1993.

30. Seymour Hersh: *The Price of Power*, New York 1983, and the interview with Hersh in *The Progressive*, October 1998.

31. Werner Biermann/Arno Klönne: *Globale Spiele*, Cologne 2001, p. 205.

32. Gerhard Feldbauer: *Agenten, Terror, Staatskomplott. Der Mord an Aldo Moro, Rote Brigaden und* CIA, Cologne, 2000.

33. Mearsheimer/Walt, p. 42f.

34. Ibid., p. 43.

35. Ibid., p. 239f.

36. Ibid., p. 239.

37. Ibid., p. 239.

38. Information from: Weichert/Zabel *Die Alpha-Journalisten*, website of Von-Halem-Verlag.

39. See 'NuoViso in conversation with Jochen Scholz', NuoViso Productions, 4 August 2009, youtube.

40. Robert Higgs: 'Who was Edward M. House?' *The Independent Review*, Vol. 13, No. 3, Winter 2009.

41. Ibid.

42. Beaudry, Vol. IV, p. 105.

43. Ibid., p. 105.

44. Ibid., see p. 105f.

45. Ibid., p. 106.

46. Ibid., p. 106.

47. Ibid., p. 106.

48. Ibid., p. 106f.

49. Ibid., p. 108.

50. Ibid., p. 108.

51. Ibid., p. 109.

52. Bilderberg Group: 'Garmisch-Partenkirchen Conference', 23–25 September 1955, Introduction, p. 1.

53. *Die Zeit*, 28.10.1977.
54. Ibid.
55. Stephen Gill: *American Hegemony and the Trilateral Commission*, Cambridge 1990.
56. von Rétyi, p. 116f.
57. Rockefeller, p. 372.
58. Ibid., p. 368f.
59. Laurence H. Shoup: 'Jimmy Carter and the Trilateralists: Presidential Roots', excerpted from the book *Trilateralism*, (p. 202) edited by Holly Sklar, South End Press, 1980.
60. Will Banyan 'The "Proud Internationalist" – The Globalist Vision of David Rockefeller', March 2006, p. 53.
61. Rockefeller, op. cit.
62. Banyan, op. cit., p. 53.
63. von Rétyi, p. 270.
64. 'Obama's Office Won't deny Senator Attended Bilderberg', (prisonplanet.com, 6.6.2008).
65. 'Leaked Agenda: Bilderberg Group Plans Economic Depression', prisonplanet.com, 6.5.2009.
66. prisonplanet.com, 6.5.2009.
67. Ibid.
68. Rétyi, p. 259.
69. Senate Report, Senate Foreign Relations Committee, 1950: 'Revision of the United Nations Charter: Hearings Before a Subcommittee of the Committee on Foreign Relations', Eighty-First Congress. United States Government Printing Office, p. 494.

# Bibliography

ALLEN, GARY: *None Dare Call It Conspiracy*, Concord Press 1972.

BEAUDRY, PIERRE: *Synarchy Movement of Empire*, Leesburg 2005, Vol. IV.

ESTULIN, DANIEL: *The True Story of the Bilderberg Group*, TrineDay, 2009.

FÜLÖP-MILLER, RENÉ: *Macht und Geheimnis der Jesuiten*, Munich 1947 [The power and secrecy of the Jesuits].

HITCHENS, CHRISTOPHER/PETER TORBERG: *The Trial of Henry Kissinger*, London 2002.

HUNTINGTON, SAMUEL: *The Soldier and the State*, Cambridge 1959.

MEARSHEIMER, JOHN/STEPHEN M. WALT: *The Israel Lobby and US Foreign Policy*, London/New York 2008.

ORWELL, GEORGE: *1984*, London 1949.

RÉTYI, ANDREAS VON: *Bilderberger – Das geheime Zentrum der Macht*, Rotterdam 2006 [Bilderbergers – the undercover centre of power].

ROCKEFELLER, DAVID: *Memoirs*, New York 2002.

# Index